Self-Help Divorce Book For Women

CRAFTED BY SKRIUWER

Copyright © 2024 by Skriuwer.

All rights reserved. No part of this book may be used or reproduced in any form whatsoever without written permission except in the case of brief quotations in critical articles or reviews.

For more information, contact : **kontakt@skriuwer.com** (www.skriuwer.com)

TABLE OF CONTENTS

CHAPTER 1: THE TRUTH ABOUT DIVORCE

- What divorce really means and why it happens
- Early steps to protect yourself
- Common emotional reactions and guilt
- Accepting the process to move forward

CHAPTER 2: SORTING OUT EMOTIONS

- Why emotions can be so strong after divorce
- Stages of grief and how they appear
- Managing anger, guilt, and shame
- Building healthier emotional habits

CHAPTER 3: BASIC LEGAL STEPS

- Filing a petition and serving the other spouse
- No-fault vs. fault divorces explained
- Spousal support and child custody basics
- Working with lawyers or representing yourself

CHAPTER 4: BUILDING A HELPFUL CIRCLE

- Why a support system matters
- Types of emotional and practical support
- Finding new resources and groups
- Setting boundaries with well-meaning friends

CHAPTER 5: PROTECTING MONEY

- Adjusting to a single-income life
- Creating a workable budget
- Spotting hidden debts or assets
- Maintaining financial security post-divorce

CHAPTER 6: HEALING THE HEART

- *Coping with deep sadness and loss*
- *Letting go of old hurts*
- *Building self-trust and closure*
- *Maintaining emotional well-being over time*

CHAPTER 7: PARENTING WITH CARE

- *Telling children about the divorce*
- *Common emotional reactions in kids*
- *Co-parenting vs. parallel parenting*
- *Helping children adjust to new routines*

CHAPTER 8: HANDLING SOCIAL STRESS

- *Announcing your divorce to others*
- *Dealing with gossip and nosey questions*
- *Attending social events with your former spouse*
- *Building new circles if old ones fade*

CHAPTER 9: GROWING SELF-WORTH

- *Difference between self-worth and self-esteem*
- *Replacing self-criticism with kindness*
- *Healthy boundaries for confidence*
- *Small actions to boost daily self-respect*

CHAPTER 10: TAKING CARE OF YOU

- *Importance of self-care routines*
- *Physical health foundations (sleep, nutrition)*
- *Simple ways to lower stress*
- *Emotional self-care and avoiding burnout*

CHAPTER 11: FINDING NEW HOBBIES

- Why hobbies help after major life change
- Indoor hobbies for creativity and relaxation
- Outdoor activities for fresh air and movement
- Balancing time for fun and responsibilities

CHAPTER 12: RE-THINKING FUTURE PLANS

- Adjusting priorities in the new phase
- Setting short-term and long-term goals
- Fear of the unknown and how to handle it
- Legal and financial aspects of new beginnings

CHAPTER 13: NAVIGATING COURT

- Understanding the courtroom setup
- Paperwork and evidence preparation
- Staying calm during cross-examination
- Dealing with rulings and next steps

CHAPTER 14: STAYING CALM

- Why calmness matters for clear thinking
- Recognizing early signs of stress
- Quick and longer-term calming techniques
- Mindset shifts to lower anxiety

CHAPTER 15: DATING SAFELY

- Checking emotional readiness for dating
- Online vs. traditional methods
- Handling first meetings with caution
- Protecting children's well-being when dating

CHAPTER 16: WORK AND CAREER

- Assessing job needs after divorce
- Updating skills or education
- Balancing work with parenting
- Building confidence and career resilience

CHAPTER 17: MAKING A NEW HOME

- Choosing where to live and budgeting
- Staying or moving from the marital home
- Personalizing your space to feel secure
- Helping children adjust to a different place

CHAPTER 18: SETTING HEALTHY BOUNDARIES

- What boundaries are and why they matter
- Signs you need clearer limits
- Communicating boundaries to ex-spouse, family, and friends
- Maintaining self-boundaries for well-being

CHAPTER 19: RENEWING CONNECTIONS

- Rebuilding ties with old friends
- Strengthening family bonds carefully
- Forming new friendships or networks
- Dealing with social anxiety and cultural barriers

CHAPTER 20: MOVING FORWARD WITH STRENGTH

- Reflecting on how far you've come
- Continuing self-care and setting fresh goals
- Nurturing work, finances, and personal growth
- Embracing a secure, confident future

CHAPTER 1

The Truth About Divorce

Divorce is the legal ending of a marriage. Many people do not think it will happen to them, but it can happen for various reasons. This chapter will talk about what divorce really is, how it happens, and why it happens. It will also show you some facts that might surprise you and give you helpful tips for coping in the early stages.

1.1 What Divorce Means

Marriage is a contract between two people. It sets out legal rights and responsibilities. When a divorce takes place, the couple decides—or a court decides—that this legal bond is over. That means each person stops being a spouse and has the right to live a separate life.

Some people feel relief when divorce starts. Others feel great sadness. Others feel both at once. There is no single way to feel, and there is no single "correct" reaction. But it helps to understand the basics of what is going on.

A Little-Known Fact:

- Sometimes, divorce can be the result of a silent problem. For example, a person might not know how to talk about money issues, and a spouse might hide debts or spend money in secret. This can create stress that builds up. People may assume that divorce happens only because of loud fights, but silent money problems can also lead to the end of a marriage.

1.2 Common Reasons for Divorce

People often think that the most common reason for divorce is fighting. Fighting is part of many separations, but there are many reasons:

1. **Lack of Communication:** When spouses do not talk about problems, the problems can grow bigger. They might pretend nothing is wrong, but the problem sits there, getting worse.
2. **Dishonesty:** Lying about money, affairs, or even small daily things can ruin trust. Trust is hard to fix once it is broken.

3. **Unmet Expectations:** Sometimes, one person has ideas about what married life should look like. If the other spouse has very different ideas, conflict can happen.
4. **Financial Stress:** Money can cause big pressures. Debts, job loss, and unexpected expenses can cause tension in the home.
5. **Changing Personal Goals:** People change over time. If two people change in ways that do not match, they may decide to split up.

None of these reasons make divorce easy or simple. But understanding why it might happen can help you realize that you are not alone. Many women feel like they failed. But in many cases, the problem has deep roots that go back years.

1.3 First Steps to Take When You Realize Divorce Is Likely

1. **Stay Safe:** If you are in a harmful situation, your safety is most important. This can mean finding a safe place to stay or getting help from a hotline.
2. **Gather Important Papers:** If you suspect that a split is near, collect birth certificates, marriage license, bank statements, credit card statements, and any records of assets. Keep them in a safe spot, possibly outside the home if you do not feel comfortable leaving them where you live.
3. **Do Not Make Rash Choices:** Big choices, such as selling property or quitting a job, should be thought through. Talk to a trusted person or a legal advisor before you act.

1.4 The Emotional Shock

Many people compare the emotional shock of divorce to the loss of a loved one. It can feel like a kind of grief. You might feel sadness, anger, fear, or even guilt. It is normal to move through these feelings at different times. Some days are better than others.

A Helpful Strategy: Keep a small notebook or use your phone to write down thoughts. Seeing your worries on paper can make them feel smaller. It can also help you track if you are stuck in a certain mood and need more help, like talking to a counselor.

1.5 The Role of Family and Friends

You might have a family that takes sides. Or you might have friends who do not know how to react. This can be stressful, but it is useful to remember:

- Not everyone will understand your reasons.
- Some people might blame you or your spouse without really knowing the full story.
- You do not have to explain every detail to everyone.

It might help to share the basics: "We have decided that our marriage is not working, and we are separating." You can add more if you choose, but you are not required to.

1.6 Dealing with Guilt

Many women feel guilty when a marriage ends. This guilt might come from personal beliefs or from society. You might think you did not try hard enough. Or you might think you failed at being a good spouse. It is important to understand that guilt can block you from moving forward. Instead of staying stuck in guilt, consider talking to a counselor or writing down reasons why the marriage did not work. You will likely see that not everything was in your control.

1.7 Facts That Might Surprise You

1. **Divorce Can Be a Financial Hit for Women More Than Men:** Studies show that women often lose financial security after a split. Sometimes women earn less or might not have the same job experience if they stayed home.
2. **Health Can Be Affected:** Stress from divorce can bring on headaches, stomach issues, and trouble sleeping.
3. **Long-Term Effects Are Not Always Negative:** In many cases, a woman finds that, over time, life can be more peaceful without the constant stress of a bad marriage.

These facts are not meant to scare you but to show that you might experience changes that need planning. If you know about these possible changes, you can get ready and protect yourself.

1.8 The Role of Hope

While divorce is hard, many women find they feel a sense of calm once the process has begun. If they were in a tense marriage, they see that life can get better. This does not mean it is all easy, but having hope is key. Hope can look like small actions, such as applying for a job, signing up for a class, or talking to someone who can give real help.

1.9 Steps to Prepare

- **Write Down Your Top Three Concerns:** This could be about money, children, living situation, or how others might treat you.
- **Gather Knowledge:** Read books, talk to legal experts, learn about your rights.
- **Look at Your Support System:** Do you have family nearby? Can you count on certain friends? Is there a local women's group or community center that can help?

1.10 Setting Realistic Expectations

One mistake people make is thinking that a divorce can be handled quickly and without any bumps. The truth is, it can take time and can be complicated. Courts have schedules, and the system can move slowly. Disagreements about property, money, and children can lead to more delays. Understanding this helps you prepare so that you are not shocked if it takes longer.

1.11 Finding Strength in the Facts

Knowledge is power. The more you learn about your situation—like how property is divided in your region, or what you can do if your spouse is hiding money—the better you can protect yourself. Use reliable sources, such as official government pages, certified counselors, or trusted authors with expertise in divorce law.

An Extra Tip: Some local courts or legal aid groups have free classes on divorce basics. They teach you about forms, court rules, and the steps in the process. This can be a huge help if you cannot afford a private lawyer right away.

1.12 Small Steps to Handle Stress

1. **Take Short Walks:** Daily short walks can calm your mind.
2. **Focus on Sleep:** If you find it hard to sleep, try an audio track with calming sounds at bedtime.

3. **Limit Harmful Talk:** Spending hours worrying or complaining can increase stress. It is good to share your feelings, but find someone who will help you think of solutions, not just feed your anger.

1.13 Why This Chapter Matters

Some people skip the early stage of accepting the divorce. They want to fast-forward to the final stage. But skipping the first steps can cause confusion. This chapter's aim was to give you a solid understanding of what divorce is, why it happens, and how to handle the first shock.

In later chapters, we will look at how to deal with many of the topics we mentioned: money, children, emotional care, and more. But for now, keep in mind that the divorce process involves legal, emotional, and practical steps.

1.14 End-of-Chapter Summary

- Divorce is the legal end of a marriage.
- It can happen because of lack of communication, dishonesty, and more.
- Early steps include protecting your personal safety and collecting important documents.
- Emotional shock is normal. Guilt is common, but often undeserved.
- Hope plays a role in moving forward.
- Having facts about the divorce process can help you feel more prepared.

CHAPTER 2

Sorting Out Emotions

When a marriage ends, the heart often goes through many strong emotions. It is normal to feel sad, angry, or confused. This chapter looks at these feelings in detail, helping you understand why they happen, and offering concrete steps to handle them. This chapter also shares helpful strategies for building a healthier mindset.

2.1 Why Emotions Can Be So Strong

Marriage is more than a piece of paper. It involves building a life with another person. When that life changes, it can feel like you are losing part of yourself. You might feel:

- **Sadness:** Grieving the loss of your shared life.
- **Anger:** Feeling upset about betrayal or broken promises.
- **Confusion:** Unsure about how you got here and what will happen next.
- **Relief:** If your marriage was full of conflict or stress, you might feel lighter.

All of these can happen at the same time, which can be overwhelming.

2.2 Stages of Emotional Recovery

Experts often list stages of grief: denial, anger, bargaining, sadness, and acceptance. You might move through these stages in a different order. You might skip some or circle back to others.

Key Point to Remember: There is no single timeline for healing. One person might feel better in a few months, while another might take a year or more. It does not mean you are weak if it takes longer.

2.3 The Anger Trap

Anger is common during divorce. You might feel angry at your spouse for breaking vows or for not working hard enough to fix problems. You might feel angry at yourself for not seeing problems sooner. While anger is normal, it can hurt you if it stays too long. Anger can lead to unwise decisions, such as sending heated messages or yelling in front of children.

How to Manage Anger:

1. **Count to Ten:** Take a pause before you respond to a text or an email.
2. **Write an Angry Letter, Then Tear It Up:** This can help release the feeling without damaging relationships or your legal case.
3. **Talk to a Counselor:** A good counselor helps you process anger in healthy ways.

2.4 Guilt and Shame

Many women feel guilt, thinking they failed as a wife or mother. Shame is deeper—it makes you think something is wrong with you as a person. This can lead to low self-esteem. To work through guilt and shame:

- **Recognize What You Can Control:** You cannot control how another person feels or acts.
- **Look at the Facts:** Were you the only reason the marriage ended? Probably not. Marriage is a two-person effort.
- **Seek Support:** Share your feelings with a trusted friend or counselor who can remind you that you are worthy of respect and kindness.

2.5 Sadness and Depression

Feeling sad or even depressed is common. You might see changes like sleeping too much, sleeping too little, losing interest in things you once liked, or feeling hopeless. It is important to note that sadness and depression are not the same. Sadness is a normal reaction that can come and go, while depression can last for weeks or months and can affect your daily life.

If you think you are depressed, you might:

1. **Talk to a Doctor:** They can check if medication or therapy is right for you.
2. **Make Small Goals:** Try to do small tasks, such as making your bed. These tiny successes can help lift your mood.
3. **Avoid Isolation:** Even if you do not feel like meeting people, a small bit of social contact can help.

2.6 Fear of the Unknown

Another big emotion is fear. You might worry about living alone or paying bills by yourself. You might fear losing friends who side with your spouse. Acknowledging that fear is normal is the first step. Then, ask yourself, "What is one small step I can take to manage this fear?" For example, if you fear money troubles, gather all your financial info and look at the numbers. Knowing the facts can reduce anxiety.

2.7 Tools to Handle Overwhelming Feelings

1. **Mood Journal:** Note what you are feeling and why. Patterns might emerge, such as feeling worse after certain triggers like phone calls with your spouse.
2. **Deep Breathing Techniques:** For instance, breathe in for four seconds, hold for four seconds, and breathe out for four seconds. This helps slow down your racing heart.
3. **Mindful Activities:** Simple tasks like coloring or doing a puzzle can bring calm because they keep your mind focused on one thing.

2.8 Handling Emotional Triggers

You might see a photo of you and your spouse from happier times. You might hear a song that reminds you of your wedding day. Such triggers can bring sudden waves of emotion. Try these strategies:

- **Put Away Old Photos:** You can store them instead of throwing them out, so you do not see them every day.
- **Make a New Playlist:** If music is a big trigger, create a fresh set of songs without shared memories.
- **Communicate Triggers to Loved Ones:** If your friends invite you to places where you spent time with your spouse, let them know you prefer a different spot until you feel ready.

2.9 Emotional Support Systems

- **Close Friends or Family:** They can listen and offer a hug.
- **Support Groups:** Some communities have groups for divorced women. Hearing from others in similar situations can help you feel less alone.

- **Online Forums:** If you are uncomfortable meeting in person, online groups can offer tips and shared experiences.
- **Therapists or Counselors:** They are trained to help you navigate strong emotions in a healthy way.

2.10 Surprising Tips for Emotional Relief

1. **Writing Letters to Yourself in the Future:** Imagine yourself one year from now. Write a letter with words of encouragement. This can help you see that current pain can change over time.
2. **Creating a "Positive Facts" List:** List truths about yourself that are good. For example, "I care about my children," or "I am strong enough to seek help." Read these facts often.
3. **Physical Release of Tension:** Doing simple exercises at home, like push-ups against a wall or basic stretches, can release tension.

2.11 Stop Comparing Yourself to Others

You might see other people who seemed to "move on" quickly. Or you might see couples who appear happy. Comparing can make you feel worse. You do not know their full story. Even if someone's life looks perfect on social media, they might be struggling too. Focus on your own path.

2.12 Planning for Emotional Ups and Downs

In the process of divorce, you might have periods where you feel confident and calm, then suddenly drop into sadness or anger. This can happen around legal deadlines, holidays, or random days when memories pop up. Make a plan:

1. **Identify Trusted People to Call:** This could be a friend, family member, or counselor.
2. **Have a Soothing Activity:** A warm bath, a calm walk, or a favorite TV show can help you relax when emotions spike.
3. **Practice Self-Talk:** Speak to yourself in a caring tone, like you would speak to a friend who is hurting.

2.13 Boundaries with Your Former Partner

During the divorce process, you may still need to talk to your spouse about finances, children, or shared property. Keeping emotional health in mind can be tricky if arguments flare up.

1. **Choose the Medium Wisely:** If phone calls always turn into fights, switch to email or text. This gives you time to calm down and respond carefully.
2. **Stay on Topic:** If you are discussing child pickup times, do not bring up old marital problems.
3. **Limit Contact:** If your marriage ended due to harm or very bad conflict, consider a mediator or a lawyer to handle most communication.

2.14 Handling Negative Self-Talk

Sometimes our biggest critic is inside our own head. You might think, "I will never be happy," or "I am not worthy of love." It is vital to recognize these thoughts as unhelpful. Try this method:

- **Name the Thought:** Say to yourself, "I notice I just thought that I am unworthy."
- **Question It:** Is this fact, or is it just a negative feeling?
- **Replace It:** What is a more balanced thought? For example, "I feel unworthy now, but I also know that I have people in my life who care about me."

2.15 Small but Powerful Actions

1. **Drink Enough Water:** Dehydration can make stress worse.
2. **Eat Balanced Meals:** Hunger can magnify worry or anger.
3. **Get Fresh Air:** Even opening a window can help if you cannot go outside.

These might seem too simple, but many people forget basic care when they are upset. Regular self-care can make it easier to face emotional challenges.

2.16 Releasing Resentment

Holding on to resentment can feel like dragging a heavy bag wherever you go. It slows your progress. One of the best gifts you can give yourself is letting go of anger toward your former partner, even if they did hurtful things. Letting go does not mean you ignore the harm or say it was okay. It means you free yourself from carrying the bitterness.

How to Let Go of Resentment:

- **Acknowledge It:** Do not pretend you are not mad. Admit the hurt.
- **Write a List of What You Can Control:** If you cannot change the past, focus on decisions in the present.
- **Seek Closure for Yourself:** This might mean writing in a journal about your feelings or talking to a counselor.

2.17 Handling Children's Emotions (If Applicable)

If you have children, they might also go through big feelings. They might blame you or your spouse. They might fear losing attention or a stable home. Chapter 7 will dive into this in detail, but for now:

- **Listen:** Let them talk without judging them.
- **Offer Assurance:** Remind them you love them and that you will still be there for them.
- **Be Honest But Age-Appropriate:** If they ask why you are divorcing, give simple, clear reasons without going into adult-level details.

2.18 Seek Professional Help When Needed

Emotional challenges can be tough. If you find you cannot function in daily life—if you are missing work, or not caring for yourself or your children—it is time to seek professional support. Therapists, doctors, and social workers can offer tools and, in some cases, medication.

A Surprising Statistic: Many people who attend therapy for divorce-related stress discover other issues that were hidden or ignored for years. Addressing these can lead to long-term relief and personal growth.

2.19 The Importance of a Supportive Environment

Sometimes friends or family can worsen your emotional state. If you have people around you who shame you, criticize you, or keep reminding you of your mistakes, it might be time to reduce contact. You need people who can listen and offer calm advice or empathy. This does not mean you cut them out forever, but you can limit how often you talk, especially during the hard phase of divorce.

2.20 Taking Control of Your Emotional Journey

Your emotional health is yours to shape. Yes, a divorce can be very painful, but the steps you take—seeking help, using stress-coping tools, keeping healthy routines—can make a big difference. Do not wait for time to do all the healing. Actively seek ways to help yourself.

2.21 End-of-Chapter Summary

- Expect to feel many emotions like anger, sadness, guilt, and fear.
- Recovery is not linear; you may move between different emotional states.
- Manage anger with safe outlets, and do not let it lead to rash actions.
- Recognize the difference between normal sadness and deeper depression.
- Fear of the unknown can be handled with planning and information.
- Build a support system: friends, family, online groups, or a counselor.
- Limit exposure to negative triggers and negative people.
- Let go of resentment to free yourself.
- Seek professional help if you find it hard to function day-to-day.

With these insights, you are better equipped to handle the waves of emotion that can arise. In the next chapters, we will look at legal basics, support systems, and practical steps to help you face the divorce process with a sense of direction and calm.

CHAPTER 3

Basic Legal Steps

When you face divorce, the legal part can feel confusing. There are many forms and rules. It can be hard to know who to trust or where to go for help. This chapter will break down the main steps. It is meant to guide you through the process in a clear way. Keep in mind that laws can vary from place to place, so you may need to check the rules in your area. The main goal of this chapter is to give you a broad picture of what to expect and how to protect yourself.

3.1 Understanding the Divorce Process

1. **Filing a Petition or Complaint:**
   In most places, one spouse has to file paperwork to start the process. This is often called a "Petition for Divorce" or a "Complaint." It states basic information: names, date of marriage, place of marriage, and why the person is seeking a divorce.
2. **Serving the Other Spouse:**
   After the form is filed, the other spouse has to be given a copy. This is called "service of process." It is an important step. If a spouse is not served correctly, it can lead to delays. In some areas, a professional server or sheriff does this. In others, you can mail the forms by certified mail.
3. **Waiting for a Response:**
   The spouse who receives the petition must respond in writing, often within a certain number of days. If they do not respond on time, the court may let the divorce go ahead without their input. This is sometimes called a "default divorce."
4. **Financial Disclosures:**
   Both spouses may have to share detailed financial information. This includes pay stubs, tax returns, bank statements, credit card bills, and any property deeds. This helps the court or mediators see what property there is and how to split it.
5. **Negotiations or Mediation:**
   Many couples try to settle issues outside of a courtroom. Mediation is when a neutral person helps both sides agree on how to handle property,

custody, and support. It can save time and money if both sides are willing to talk calmly.
6. **Court Hearings (If Needed):**
If no agreement can be reached, a judge will hear each side's arguments. The judge then decides about property, money support, and child-related issues.
7. **Final Decree:**
Once everything is decided, the judge signs a final decree or judgment. This is the official end of the marriage in the eyes of the law.

3.2 No-Fault vs. Fault Divorce

Different areas have different divorce laws. Some places allow "no-fault divorce." That means you do not have to prove your spouse did anything wrong. You can simply state the marriage cannot be fixed. Other places still allow "fault" grounds, where one person argues the other spouse did something major (like cruelty or adultery) to cause the marriage to fail.

- **No-Fault Divorce:** Often faster and less dramatic.
- **Fault Divorce:** Can require more proof and can lead to longer court battles.

If your area has a no-fault option, many people choose it to reduce arguments, even if they feel the other spouse was at fault. That choice can lower legal costs and stress.

3.3 Spousal Support (Alimony)

Spousal support (sometimes called alimony) is money paid by one spouse to the other after the marriage ends. It can help a spouse with lower earnings maintain a decent standard of living.

1. **Types of Support:**
    - **Temporary Support:** This is for the time during the divorce process.

- **Long-Term Support:** This might go on for a set number of years. In some rare cases, it can be lifelong, but that depends on local law and the length of the marriage.
    - **Rehabilitative Support:** Money paid for a while so the spouse can get training or education to support themselves.
2. **How Courts Decide:**
    - Length of the marriage
    - Each spouse's job skills and education
    - Health and age
    - What each spouse can earn now and in the future

If you think you might need spousal support, gather evidence of your living costs, job history, and your spouse's income. A lawyer can help you present a solid case to the court or use this info in negotiations.

3.4 Child Custody and Support (If Children Are Involved)

If you have children, deciding who they will live with is a big concern. There are different forms of custody:

- **Physical Custody:** Where the child lives most of the time.
- **Legal Custody:** Who makes decisions about the child's health, education, and welfare.

Courts tend to favor arrangements that keep both parents involved if possible, unless one parent is harmful. Child support is money to help cover the costs of raising a child. The exact amount depends on laws in your area, each parent's income, and the child's needs.

A Key Point to Remember:
Child support is the child's right, not the parent's. A parent cannot choose to "give it up." The money is for the child's care.

3.5 Division of Property

When two people end a marriage, the court or mediators have to split what they own. This can include the house, cars, furniture, and even debts. Property can be:

- **Marital Property:** Anything earned or bought during the marriage.
- **Separate Property:** Anything owned by a spouse before the marriage or received as a gift or inheritance.

Community Property States: Some places follow "community property" rules. That often means all marital property is split 50-50.

Equitable Distribution States: Other places follow "equitable distribution," which tries to split property in a fair way, not always 50-50.

3.6 Working with Lawyers

1. **Finding the Right Lawyer:**
   Ask friends or family for recommendations. Check local bar associations. Make sure the lawyer has experience with divorce cases.
2. **Cost:**
   Lawyers can be expensive. Ask how they bill—hourly, a flat fee, or a retainer.
3. **Communication Style:**
   Some lawyers prefer email, others prefer phone calls. Ask how they handle updates so you do not feel out of the loop.
4. **Questions to Ask:**
   - How many cases like mine have you handled?
   - How often will we communicate?
   - Do you foresee any major problems with my case?

If you cannot afford a private lawyer, look for legal aid services or pro bono programs in your area.

3.7 Self-Representation (If You Cannot Hire a Lawyer)

Some people decide to represent themselves in court. This is known as being a "pro se" litigant. If you choose this route:

1. **Learn the Rules:** Courts have specific procedures for filing documents and speaking in front of a judge. You need to follow these rules carefully.
2. **Stay Organized:** Keep track of deadlines, forms, and any evidence you want to present.
3. **Look for Workshops:** Many courts offer free or low-cost workshops to guide you through the basics of filing for divorce.
4. **Respect the Court:** Dressing appropriately and speaking politely can help the judge see you as a serious individual.

A Caution: If your case is complicated—maybe involving kids, property, or possible hidden assets—having a lawyer is often a safer choice if you can manage it.

3.8 Mediation vs. Litigation

- **Mediation:** A neutral person works with both spouses to reach agreements. Mediation can be cheaper and faster than a court trial. It also tends to create less conflict. However, it depends on both parties being willing to cooperate.
- **Litigation:** This involves going to court, presenting evidence to a judge, and sometimes having a jury (though that is less common in divorce). Litigation can be lengthy and costly. It can also fuel more tension. But if you cannot reach an agreement through talks or if the other person is unreasonable, litigation might be the only way to solve it.

3.9 Protective Orders (If Safety Is a Concern)

In some marriages, a spouse might feel unsafe. If there is any threat of harm, you have the right to seek a protective or restraining order. This can:

- Stop the other person from contacting you or coming near you

- Protect children if they are also at risk

If you need this, reach out to a local domestic harm hotline or a shelter. They can guide you on how to get an order quickly.

3.10 Gathering Evidence

You might not think of divorce as a place where "evidence" is needed, but it can matter. Examples include:

- **Texts or Emails:** If they show harassment, threats, or hidden deals.
- **Financial Records:** To prove your spouse has hidden money or has large debts.
- **Witness Statements:** Friends or family might have seen how your spouse behaves.

Never fake or change documents. That can harm your credibility. Instead, keep everything in an organized folder, sorted by date.

3.11 Handling Court Deadlines

Courts usually set deadlines for each step, such as:

- Filing a response
- Handing over financial documents
- Scheduling mediation or court appearances

Missing a deadline can hurt your case. If you have a lawyer, they usually track these dates for you. If you are on your own, mark all deadlines on a calendar and set reminders on your phone.

3.12 Surprising Facts about Legal Fees

- **Retainer Fees:** Many lawyers ask for an upfront payment (retainer) that they bill from as they work.

- **Some Firms Offer Payment Plans:** If you ask, some may let you pay in installments.
- **Legal Insurance:** A few people have coverage through their job or a professional organization. It might cover part of the cost of a lawyer.

It is wise to speak openly about costs. If you cannot afford a private attorney, do not be shy about checking if a lawyer can work out a payment plan or if you can get help from legal aid.

3.13 Being Smart with Social Media

In a divorce, anything you post online can be used against you. If you post about taking a vacation or buying new items, the other side might claim you have more money than you say. If you post angry comments about your spouse, it might damage your case.

A Good Rule:
Keep personal details offline, at least until the case ends. Some lawyers advise clients to stop using social media entirely during the process or to set accounts to private. Even then, be cautious because friends might share your posts.

3.14 Avoiding Common Mistakes

1. **Hiding Assets:** Some people think they can "hide" bank accounts or property. Courts take this very seriously. If caught, you can lose trust and face penalties.
2. **Letting Emotions Rule:** Yelling in court or writing angry emails can harm your case. Courts like calm, logical actions.
3. **Bad-Mouthing the Other Parent (If Kids Are Involved):** Judges do not like to see a parent who tries to turn children against the other parent. It can backfire.
4. **Skipping Court Dates:** If you fail to appear, the judge might make rulings without hearing your side.

3.15 Lesser-Known Tips for Legal Protection

- **Review of Prenuptial or Postnuptial Agreements:** If you have one, do not forget it. It might affect property division.
- **Credit Report Checks:** Your spouse might open credit cards without your knowledge. Check your report regularly.
- **Separate Your Bank Accounts Early (If Safe to Do So):** If you know a split is likely, open an account in your name only. This helps protect your income from being drained by the other spouse.
- **Life Insurance Policies:** Sometimes, a divorce settlement includes who pays for or benefits from life insurance. This can matter if you have children.

3.16 Courtroom Behavior (If You Must Appear)

If you do go to court:

- **Dress Modestly:** You do not have to buy an expensive suit, but aim for neat, clean clothes.
- **Speak Clearly:** Answer the judge's questions with short, direct answers.
- **Do Not Interrupt:** Even if you disagree, wait for your turn.
- **Show Respect:** Use "Yes, Your Honor" or "No, Your Honor" where needed.

These small details can shape how the judge views you.

3.17 Documents You Should Keep

A divorce case can produce a lot of paperwork. Keep the following:

- Filed petitions or complaints
- Responses from your spouse
- Court orders, temporary or final
- Financial disclosures (yours and your spouse's)
- Child custody agreements, if any
- Spousal support agreements, if any

Also save copies of emails or letters from your lawyer, or from your spouse's lawyer, as well as any mediation agreements. Keep them in one place so you can refer to them easily.

3.18 Communication with Your Spouse's Lawyer

In many divorce situations, you might need to speak or write to your spouse's lawyer. Remember:

- **Stay Calm:** They are not your friend, but they are also not your enemy. They are doing their job.
- **Keep It Short:** Respond to questions clearly without sharing extra details.
- **Never Lie:** If you are caught lying, it will seriously damage your credibility.

If you have a lawyer, often your lawyer will handle communication for you. If you are on your own, be firm but polite.

3.19 Final Checks Before Court Settlement

If you come to an agreement before a trial:

1. **Read It Carefully:** Once you sign, it can be hard to change.
2. **Check the Numbers:** Make sure child support or spousal support amounts are correct.
3. **Talk to a Financial Advisor:** If the agreement involves splitting retirement accounts or the house, see how it affects your long-term finances.

This step is crucial because a divorce settlement might affect your life for years. It is a good idea to have a professional review it if you can afford to.

3.20 Life After the Final Decree

Once the divorce is finalized, you will get a final order or decree. This order can cover child custody, support, property division, and more. Keep a certified copy in a safe place. In some areas, you may need to update your name on your driver's license or with Social Security if you changed your name. You might also need to update beneficiaries on life insurance or retirement accounts.

A Surprising Note: Sometimes, even after the final decree, people go back to court to change parts of it. For instance, if you lose your job, you might ask to lower child support. Or if your spouse gets a huge pay increase, you might ask for a modification.

3.21 End-of-Chapter Summary

- **Filing and Serving:** The first legal steps are submitting a petition and giving the other spouse proper notice.
- **Financial Disclosures:** Both spouses need to share details on income and assets.
- **Spousal and Child Support:** Courts look at factors like length of marriage, each person's income, and children's needs.
- **Property Division:** Marital property gets split based on local rules.
- **Lawyers and Costs:** Hiring a good lawyer can help, but there are lower-cost options for those who cannot afford private attorneys.
- **Mediation vs. Litigation:** Mediation can be cheaper and kinder, but sometimes a court case is needed.
- **Courtroom Tips:** Dress and act respectfully.
- **After the Final Decree:** Make sure you update your documents and accounts.

With this overview, you have a clearer sense of what the legal process might look like. In the next chapter, we will look at building a circle of support—friends, family, experts—who can help you handle not just the legal side, but also the emotional and practical sides of divorce.

CHAPTER 4

Building a Helpful Circle

A divorce can feel like you are going through it all by yourself. Friends, family, and other people can help, but it is normal to feel unsure about who to reach out to. This chapter focuses on building a circle of people and resources who can provide real assistance. This includes emotional support, practical help, and professional guidance. Having the right people by your side can make a big difference in how you handle each step.

4.1 Why a Support System Matters

Going through a divorce can bring stress and worry. You may feel lost or scared. A helpful circle can:

- Remind you that you are not alone
- Offer ideas or resources you did not know about
- Provide a sense of comfort and routine
- Help you see new possibilities

One challenge is that some friends or relatives might take sides or offer unhelpful advice. That is why you need to build a circle that is balanced, stable, and truly caring.

4.2 Types of Support

1. **Emotional Support:**
   These are people who can listen without judging, who let you cry if you need to, and who do not push you to do things you are not ready for. They might be close friends, siblings, or a counselor.
2. **Practical Support:**
   These people help with day-to-day tasks, like babysitting, cooking a meal, or giving you a ride to court if your car is in the shop. They might be neighbors, coworkers, or extended family.

3. **Expert Support:**
   Lawyers, counselors, financial advisors, or religious leaders (if relevant to your life). Their guidance can save you time and stress because they know how to handle specific problems.

4.3 Checking Your Current Circle

Before you add new people to your circle, look at who is already in your life:

- **Who do you trust the most?**
- **Who usually helps you think clearly?**
- **Who has proven reliable in tough times?**

Some people might surprise you. Maybe a coworker you do not know very well is actually very resourceful. On the other hand, a longtime friend might be too negative or might cause drama. It is okay to accept help from some people and avoid it from others.

4.4 Setting Boundaries

During a divorce, some well-meaning friends and family might ask too many questions or push advice on you. They might say, "You should do this," or "Why did you do that?" or "I think you're making a big mistake."

Ways to Set Boundaries Politely:

- "I appreciate your concern, but I would rather not go into details."
- "Thank you for offering advice, but I already have a plan in place."
- "I know you care about me, and I'll let you know if I need more input."

It can be hard to be firm, especially if this person is a parent or older relative. Still, you have the right to decide how much you share and how much advice you accept.

4.5 How to Find New Support

1. **Support Groups:**
   Many communities have divorce support groups, sometimes hosted by churches, community centers, or counseling offices. People there understand what you are facing.
2. **Online Communities:**
   If you prefer privacy, you can join online forums or social media groups. Make sure the group is moderated and feels safe.
3. **Counselors and Therapists:**
   These professionals are trained to give you emotional tools and to help you manage stress.
4. **Workplace Resources:**
   Some employers offer Employee Assistance Programs that include free or low-cost counseling or legal guidance.

4.6 Building a Relationship with a Counselor

Some people worry that seeking a counselor means they are weak. This is not true. A counselor can help you:

- Sort out your feelings
- Handle stress in a healthier way
- Develop strategies for dealing with conflict
- Plan for the future

When looking for a counselor, check if they have experience with divorce or family issues. Ask about costs and whether they take your insurance (if you have it). If money is tight, some counselors offer sliding-scale fees based on your income.

4.7 Talking to Children About Divorce (If Applicable)

While a full discussion on parenting will come later, children can be part of your support circle in small ways. They do not have to be "grown-ups," but they do affect your emotional life. If you keep an open, honest line of communication with them, it might reduce household tension. Let them know:

- They are not to blame
- You love them no matter what
- They can ask questions about what will happen next

In return, they might show you small acts of care. But remember, they are kids. They should not bear adult problems. Seek adult support for adult problems.

4.8 Helpful Family Members vs. Harmful Family Members

Not all family is helpful. Some relatives might spread rumors, shame you, or keep asking for gossip. Others might bring kindness. You have the right to decide who is in your inner circle. Be ready for the fact that some relatives might be offended if you do not share details. But you can kindly let them know you need to limit your communication to protect your mental health.

4.9 Friends in Common with Your Spouse

One tricky part is dealing with friends you shared as a couple. Some friends might feel like they have to pick a side. Others might want to stay neutral. If you think certain mutual friends might gossip to your spouse, be cautious about sharing personal details. That does not mean you have to cut them off, but you can be mindful about the topics you discuss.

4.10 Spiritual or Religious Groups

If you have a faith community, they might offer comfort during this time. Some places have ministries or groups that support people facing personal crises. You do not have to be deeply religious to benefit from a caring group. However, if the culture of that community is judgmental about divorce, it might add stress. Seek out members who are open-minded.

4.11 Financial Advisors and Accountants

Divorce can bring large money changes. An accountant or financial advisor can help you:

- Understand taxes after divorce
- Plan a new budget
- Check if you need to adjust retirement savings
- Protect any assets you receive in the settlement

You do not need to be rich to seek this help. Even a one-time consultation can teach you important facts. Some nonprofits offer free or low-cost financial counseling.

4.12 Mentors or Role Models

Think of someone you know (or know about) who has been through a successful split and has come out okay. They do not have to be a celebrity. They could be a neighbor or a coworker. If they are open to talking, ask them how they handled tough moments. You might pick up tips or just feel more hopeful seeing that someone else managed to get through a hard situation.

4.13 Using Technology for Support

Technology can help you connect in positive ways:

- **Video Chats:** Stay in touch with friends or family who live far away.
- **Online Therapy:** Some counselors offer video sessions, which can be easier if you have a busy schedule or no childcare.
- **Apps for Mood Tracking:** Apps can help you log emotions, remind you to breathe or rest, and even connect you with a support group.

Just be careful about sharing sensitive information online. Use secure platforms and privacy settings where possible.

4.14 Support in the Workplace

If you are working, your boss or coworkers may notice changes in your mood or schedule. Decide how much you want to share. In some jobs, it might help to tell your boss you are going through a divorce, so they understand if you need time off for court dates. Many companies have human resources staff who can direct you to counseling or mediation services.

4.15 Helping Others Help You

Sometimes, people want to support you but do not know how. They might say, "Let me know if you need anything." You can guide them:

- Be specific: "I have a court date next Tuesday. Could you watch my child for two hours?"
- Ask for help with tasks you find draining: "I'm feeling overwhelmed. Could you help me fold laundry or cook a simple meal?"
- Let them know it is okay if they cannot help with everything.

By being clear, you reduce confusion and avoid situations where friends say they will help but never do anything.

4.16 Avoiding Too Many Cooks in the Kitchen

While support is good, too many opinions can confuse you. If you share every detail of your divorce with multiple people, you might get conflicting advice. Choose a small group of trusted advisors—a lawyer, a counselor, a close friend. Then kindly thank others for caring but explain you have it handled.

4.17 Handling Gossip

Unfortunately, people sometimes talk about other people's private lives. If you find out someone is spreading rumors about you or your spouse, it can hurt. Decide if it is worth confronting the person. Often, ignoring gossip is best. If a coworker or family member is repeating false statements, you can calmly correct them if you want to. But do not let it consume your energy. Focus on people and places where you feel safe.

4.18 Maintaining Your Independence

A support system does not mean you rely on others for every little thing. It is about having help so you can stand strong on your own. If a friend or family member starts making decisions for you or starts controlling your finances, that can be a red flag. Stay aware of whether your helpers are truly supporting you or trying to control your life.

4.19 Surprising Ways to Gain Support

- **Local Community Classes:** Taking a cooking or fitness class can help you meet new people and get your mind off stress.
- **Volunteer Work:** Helping others can bring a sense of purpose. You might meet kind-hearted people who share your values.
- **Parent-Teacher Associations (If You Have Kids):** School groups can introduce you to other parents who understand the challenges of family life.

4.20 Putting It All Together

Building a helpful circle is like creating a patchwork of different people with different strengths. One friend might be good at cheering you up when you feel down. Another might be great at practical errands. A counselor can handle the deep emotional issues. A lawyer can handle legal needs. You do not have to rely on one person for everything.

Things to Remember:

- Not everyone in your circle has to be a close friend. Some might just be there for a specific purpose, like legal help or babysitting.

- You can be honest about what you can handle. If you need space, say so.
- You can reduce contact with people who are draining or negative.

4.21 End-of-Chapter Summary

- **Why Support Matters:** It helps with stress, offers new ideas, and helps you feel less alone.
- **Types of Support:** Emotional, practical, and expert help all have their place.
- **Checking Your Circle:** Identify who you trust and who helps you think clearly.
- **Setting Boundaries:** You do not have to share everything with everyone.
- **Finding New Resources:** Support groups, online communities, and counselors are good starting points.
- **Helping Others Help You:** Be specific about what you need so people can truly assist you.
- **Avoiding Gossip:** Do not let rumors take up your energy.
- **Maintaining Independence:** A support system should help you grow stronger, not control you.

By filling your life with people who genuinely care and offer useful help, you build a safety net. This circle will make it easier to handle the legal and emotional sides of your divorce. In the next chapters, we will talk about protecting your finances, healing your emotional wounds, and parenting with care, among other important topics.

CHAPTER 5

Protecting Money

Money plays a major role in divorce. You might worry about how to pay bills or if you can keep your home. You might fear your spouse will hide assets. It is normal to feel uncertain. This chapter will give you detailed methods to protect what you have, plan for the future, and avoid common traps. By getting organized and learning about money rules, you can stand on firmer ground.

5.1 Shifts in Financial Life After Divorce

When a marriage ends, your money situation changes. You go from a two-person setup to a single-person budget (or single parent budget if kids are involved). You might see:

1. **Less Income:** If both spouses worked and pooled money, now you have only your paycheck or only part of what you used to share.
2. **Changed Expenses:** You may pay rent or a mortgage alone. You may handle costs that your spouse used to cover.
3. **Possible Legal Fees:** Divorce can include lawyer bills, court costs, and more.

This shift can be scary, but you can get through it with planning. The first step is to look at where your money is coming from and where it is going.

5.2 Making a New Budget

A budget is a plan for how you use your money. It does not have to be fancy. You can write it on a piece of paper or use a simple phone app.

1. **List Your Income:**
    - Salary or wages from your job
    - Child support or spousal support (if applicable)
    - Side jobs, freelance, or part-time work
    - Any public benefits

2. **List All Expenses:**
    - Rent or mortgage
    - Utilities (electricity, water, gas, internet)
    - Food
    - Childcare, if you have kids
    - Insurance (health, car, home)
    - Car payments, gas, or public transport costs
    - Credit card bills
    - Medical costs
    - Personal items (clothes, grooming)
    - Entertainment (streaming services, outings)
3. **Compare:**
   Subtract expenses from income. If you end up with a negative amount, you need to cut costs or bring in more money.
4. **Adjust:**
   Maybe you can downgrade your phone plan, or switch to cooking at home more often, or pick up extra hours at work.

A budget is not punishment. It is a clear view of your money so you can make informed choices.

5.3 Looking for Hidden Debts or Assets

In some divorces, a spouse might have debts you never knew about. Or they might hide money in a separate account.

Steps to Stay Alert:

1. **Check Your Credit Report:** You can get a free copy each year. Look for any unfamiliar loans or credit cards.
2. **Look at Bank Statements:** If you see strange transfers, ask for explanations.
3. **Ask for Full Financial Disclosure:** In many places, the law says both spouses must share their financial details during divorce.

If you suspect hidden assets, share that concern with your lawyer. They may hire a financial investigator or subpoena bank records. Do not ignore odd activity.

5.4 Dealing with Joint Accounts

Many married couples have joint checking or savings accounts. Once you know divorce is likely, think about how to protect that money.

1. **Open Your Own Account:** Put some money in it so you have funds that only you can access.
2. **Talk to the Bank (If Safe):** Let them know there is a pending divorce. In some places, you can ask the bank to require two signatures before big withdrawals.
3. **Check Bank Policies:** If your spouse empties the account, you may have legal options. But prevention is best.

Be wise about closing accounts. If you close them all at once, it can spark conflict. Aim for a balanced approach.

5.5 Credit Scores and Loans

Your credit score is an important measure of how you handle debt. A good credit score can help you get better interest rates. During divorce, watch out for changes that might damage your credit:

1. **Joint Credit Cards:** If both names are on the card, late payments or high balances affect you.
2. **Removing an Authorized User:** If your spouse is just an authorized user on your card, you can ask the credit company to remove them if needed.
3. **Mortgage Loans:** If both names are on the home loan, you might need to refinance to remove one name.

Keep an eye on your credit report. Do not wait until the end of the divorce to see what shape it is in.

5.6 Understanding Taxes After Divorce

Taxes can become more complex when you split up:

1. **Filing Status:** If your divorce is final before December 31, you usually file as single or head of household (if you have kids and qualify). If still married on December 31, you might have to file as married.

2. **Child-Related Credits:** Decide who claims the child as a dependent. Sometimes this is agreed upon in the divorce settlement.
3. **Spousal Support:** In some places, if you receive spousal support, it might not be taxed as it once was. The rules changed in certain regions, so check the updated law in your area.

If you are confused, see a tax professional. Making a mistake can cost you later.

5.7 Retirement Accounts and Investments

Many people forget about retirement savings during a divorce, or they think they will deal with it later. But these accounts can be quite valuable.

1. **401(k) or Pension Plans:** If contributions happened while married, that portion might be considered marital property.
2. **IRAs (Individual Retirement Accounts):** Similar rules apply.
3. **Stocks or Bonds:** If you and your spouse invested together, the value may need to be split.

You might need something called a Qualified Domestic Relations Order (QDRO) to split retirement funds without penalties or tax hits. A lawyer who knows about retirement assets can help you get this right.

5.8 Future Earning Potential

Sometimes, one spouse has a greater chance of earning more money in the future. Maybe they have a higher level of education or a stable job with benefits. In some areas, this factor is considered when awarding spousal support or dividing property.

- If you stayed at home or worked part-time, it might be wise to look at ways to improve your earning power. This could mean taking classes, earning a certificate, or updating your resume.
- If your spouse has big earning potential, a court might grant more spousal support for a set period, especially if you need time to train for a job.

5.9 If Your Spouse Handled All the Finances

In many marriages, one person handles the money. If that was your spouse, you might feel lost. You can still protect yourself:

1. **Gather Records:** Ask for bank statements, credit card bills, tax returns, pay stubs, insurance policies, retirement account statements.
2. **Use Online Tools:** Many banks have online tutorials about budgeting, saving, and investing basics.
3. **Meet with a Financial Coach:** Even a one-time appointment can help you see how to manage bills and plan.

Feeling embarrassed is normal, but learning is possible at any stage of life.

5.10 Ways to Save on Legal Fees

Divorce can get expensive if you are not careful. Here are ways to keep costs under control:

1. **Get Organized:** Keep your documents in one place. When you meet your lawyer, have a clear list of questions. This saves time.
2. **Try Mediation First:** If you can solve disputes calmly with a mediator, you might avoid a long court battle.
3. **Use Email Wisely:** Lawyers often bill by the hour. Constant phone calls can raise your bill. Email can be more efficient, but keep it brief and focused.
4. **Ask About Payment Plans:** Some law firms allow you to pay over time.

5.11 Practical Ways to Stretch Money

1. **Meal Planning:**
    - Write a weekly menu and buy groceries based on that plan.
    - Cook larger meals and freeze leftovers.
2. **Cut Monthly Subscriptions:**
    - Check for services you rarely use.
    - Cancel or pause them during the divorce process.

3. **Carpool or Public Transit:**
   - If you can share rides, you might save on gas and reduce car wear.
4. **Take Advantage of Secondhand Shops:**
   - Clothes, furniture, or appliances can be cheaper when gently used.

These changes might feel small, but they add up over time.

5.12 Avoiding Common Money Mistakes

1. **Emotional Spending:**
   During stressful times, some people shop to feel better. But debt can grow quickly.
2. **Not Tracking Shared Bills:**
   If you and your spouse still share certain bills (like a mortgage) while separated, make sure payments are being made on time.
3. **Co-Signing New Loans:**
   Do not co-sign anything for your spouse once you know a divorce is happening. You could get stuck with the debt if they do not pay.
4. **Ignoring Health Insurance:**
   If you are covered under your spouse's health plan, find out when that coverage ends and what your choices are for new insurance.

5.13 Checking for Government or Community Assistance

If money is very tight, you might qualify for help:

1. **Housing Assistance:** Some areas have programs that help with rent or utilities.
2. **Food Assistance:** Options like SNAP (Supplemental Nutrition Assistance Program) or local food banks.
3. **Legal Aid:** Low-income individuals might get free or reduced legal services.
4. **Job Training Programs:** Local community centers or government offices might have courses to improve your skills.

Asking for help is not a sign of weakness. These programs exist to support people in need.

5.14 Steps to Rebuild Your Finances

If your finances were ruined during marriage or you had little savings, consider these steps:

1. **Set a Savings Goal:** Even if it is just a small amount each month, watch your emergency fund grow over time.
2. **Negotiate Bills:** Call phone or cable companies to see if you can lower rates. You might be surprised how often they reduce fees if you ask.
3. **Get a Side Gig:** If you have skills like writing, tutoring, or babysitting, you can earn extra money on weekends or evenings.
4. **Use Cash When Possible:** This helps avoid credit card debt.

No single trick is magic, but consistent small steps can build a stronger foundation.

5.15 Keeping Good Records

Keep proof of all financial transactions. This can help in two ways:

1. **Legal Protection:** If your spouse claims you did not pay a bill, you have receipts.
2. **Personal Organization:** You can see how much you spend each month and plan better.

Use a folder or a simple filing system. If possible, back up digital copies on a secure cloud or external drive.

5.16 Real Estate Concerns

If you own a home together, you need to decide what happens to it:

1. **Sell and Split the Money:** This is often the simplest choice if neither person can afford the mortgage alone.
2. **One Person Buys Out the Other:** If one spouse wants to keep the house, they pay the other spouse's share of the equity.
3. **Continue Co-Owning Temporarily:** In some cases, you both keep ownership until the market improves or until the kids are grown.

Before you decide, think about costs like property taxes, maintenance, and insurance. A house can be a burden if you cannot afford it alone.

5.17 Temporary Financial Solutions

During separation, you might have temporary court orders:

- **Temporary Spousal Support:** If you need funds to get by until the final settlement.
- **Temporary Child Support:** Helps cover kids' expenses right away.
- **Frozen Accounts:** Sometimes a judge orders that no large changes can be made to joint accounts or property until the divorce is final.

If you need immediate help, talk to a lawyer about requesting these orders. They can keep you afloat if your spouse stops paying bills or tries to move assets.

5.18 Cash Flow vs. Net Worth

It is helpful to know the difference:

- **Cash Flow:** Money that comes in and goes out each month. It affects how well you can pay bills right now.
- **Net Worth:** The total of your assets (money, property, investments) minus your debts.

Divorce can change both. A person might have decent net worth (like a share in a house) but poor monthly cash flow (little money to pay bills every month). Be mindful of both short-term and long-term financial health when negotiating.

5.19 Negotiating a Fair Settlement

If you and your spouse aim to avoid court:

1. **List All Assets and Debts:** House, cars, credit cards, personal loans, retirement accounts, etc.

2. **Agree on Splits That Make Sense:** Maybe you keep more liquid money (cash) while your spouse gets more of the retirement accounts, or vice versa.
3. **Check the Tax Impact:** Some assets have taxes attached when sold or cashed in.
4. **Seek a Mediator or Lawyer to Review:** Make sure the agreement is fair and follows local laws.

5.20 End-of-Chapter Summary

- **Expect Financial Shifts:** You are moving from a shared income/expense system to handling everything alone.
- **Create a Simple Budget:** This helps you see where you stand each month.
- **Watch for Hidden Assets or Debts:** Keep an eye on your credit report and bank statements.
- **Joint Accounts:** Consider opening an account in your own name to protect funds.
- **Credit Scores and Taxes:** Understand how divorce affects both.
- **Retirement and Future Earning Potential:** Do not ignore long-term money issues.
- **Learn if You Are New to Handling Money:** Gather records, speak to a financial coach, or use online tools.
- **Mediation Can Save Legal Costs:** Being organized can also help.
- **Use Community Resources:** Food aid, job training, or housing support can make a difference.
- **Document Everything:** Good records help in legal matters and personal planning.

Protecting your money is not about being greedy or hostile. It is about ensuring you have the resources to move ahead. You want to be able to support yourself (and your children, if you have them) and avoid being caught off guard by debts or legal surprises. In the next chapter, we will look at "Healing the Heart," focusing on deeper emotional care after taking some of these practical steps for financial security.

CHAPTER 6

Healing the Heart

Divorce is not just a legal or financial event. It is also an emotional earthquake. You might feel sorrow, anger, shame, or confusion. While Chapter 2 explored sorting out emotions, this chapter dives deeper into real healing. Healing the heart goes beyond getting through day-to-day tasks. It is about finding ways to care for yourself at a deeper level.

6.1 What Is Emotional Healing?

Healing means reducing pain over time. It is not about forgetting everything that happened. It is about learning to live and move forward without the heavy weight of sadness or anger holding you down. Healing involves:

- Letting go of blame for yourself or your spouse
- Finding healthy ways to handle regret or sadness
- Developing habits that support long-term emotional balance

It can take months or even years, and that is okay.

6.2 Recognizing Grief

Ending a marriage can feel like a loss similar to death. You lose the life you knew, the plans you had, and the routines you once followed. It is normal to grieve. Grief can have stages:

1. **Shock or Numbness:** Feeling disconnected, as if this is not real.
2. **Pain or Anger:** Feeling deep hurt, rage, or regret.
3. **Sadness or Depression:** Struggling to see hope in the future.
4. **Adjustment:** Gradually starting to accept that your life has changed.
5. **Rebuilding:** Finding new ways to live and care about yourself.

You might move through these stages in a different order, or revisit some stages over time.

6.3 Practical Steps to Boost Emotional Well-Being

1. **Design a Calming Routine:**
   - Pick a consistent bedtime if possible.
   - Spend a few minutes each morning just breathing quietly before checking your phone or starting your tasks.
2. **Check In with Yourself:**
   - Once or twice a day, stop and ask, "How do I feel right now?"
   - If you feel upset, see if there is a small thing you can do—like taking a short break or writing a few notes in a journal.
3. **Limit Negative Media:**
   - Watching or reading too much stressful content can add to your worries.
   - Pick shows or news sources that do not worsen your mood.

6.4 Letting Go of Old Hurts

When trust is broken, it can leave deep wounds. Letting go of old hurts does not mean saying what happened was fine. It means choosing not to carry that pain every day.

Methods to Help:

- Write letters (you do not have to send them) that express what you feel.
- Speak to a counselor or a trusted friend about your pain.
- Practice reframing: Instead of thinking "He ruined my life," think "My life took a different direction, and I will work on improving it."

Letting go can be a repeated process. You might feel okay one day and angry the next. This is normal.

6.5 Building Self-Trust

Some people lose trust in themselves after divorce. They think, "How did I pick the wrong person?" or "Why did I let this go on so long?" To rebuild self-trust:

1. **Recognize That You Grow Over Time:** Maybe you did the best you could with the knowledge you had back then.
2. **Take Small Risks:** Try a new hobby or explore a different skill. Each success, even small, reminds you that you can depend on yourself.
3. **Use Positive Self-Talk:** When you make a mistake, say, "I made a mistake, but I can learn from it."

6.6 Seeking Closure

Closure is the sense of having some final understanding or acceptance of what happened. You might not get closure by talking to your ex-spouse. They might not want to cooperate, or they might not see the events the same way you do. You can find closure on your own.

- **Write Your Own Account:** Some people write a short personal essay about their version of the marriage's story. This helps process thoughts.
- **Symbolic Gestures:** Some folks remove wedding photos from their main living space or put them in storage. Others might give back gifts or keep them in a box out of sight.
- **Ceremonies for Yourself:** Light a candle or do another small activity to mark the transition.

These might sound simple, but they can help your mind feel like it is turning a page.

6.7 Anxiety About the Future

Anxiety can flare up after divorce because so much feels new. You might worry about money, raising kids alone, or even just being by yourself.

Ways to Reduce Anxiety:

1. **Focus on What You Control:** Make a list of what is in your power (like how you spend your free time, where you apply for work) vs. what is not (like what your ex-spouse does).
2. **Practice Relaxation:** Listen to calming music, do gentle stretches, or use deep breathing.

3. **Seek Information:** If you fear you cannot manage finances, read books or watch short tutorials to learn how. Information often cuts down fear.

6.8 Rebuilding Self-Esteem

A tough divorce can dent your confidence. You might feel unwanted or think you are not good enough. To rebuild:

1. **List Your Good Points:** Do this weekly. Include anything from kindness to problem-solving.
2. **Find Supportive Groups:** People who say kind, helpful things can boost your sense of worth.
3. **Set Tiny Goals and Achieve Them:** This could be organizing a drawer, finishing a short online course, or going for a daily walk. Each achievement reminds you that you can succeed.

6.9 Physical Wellness and Emotional Health

Mind and body are connected. When you care for your body, your mind often feels better too.

- **Exercise:** You do not need a gym membership. Simple walks, home exercise videos, or dancing in your living room can help.
- **Healthy Eating:** Try to include fruits, veggies, and protein. If you struggle, aim for small improvements rather than a full overhaul.
- **Sleep Habits:** Avoid screens for 30 minutes before bed if you can. Try a calming herbal tea or relaxing music.

When your body feels better, your emotional stamina can increase.

6.10 Steering Clear of Harmful Behaviors

Under stress, some people turn to habits that can hurt them over time:

- **Drinking Too Much:** It might numb pain temporarily, but it can lead to bigger problems.
- **Misusing Medication:** Always follow medical advice. Taking extra pills to sleep or relax can create harmful cycles.
- **Compulsive Behaviors (Gambling, Shopping, Overeating):** These can drain finances or hurt your health.

If you notice these issues, talk to a counselor or a support group. Early help can stop a bad habit from getting worse.

6.11 Forgiving Yourself

Guilt can weigh heavily on many women after a divorce. You might think, "I should have tried harder," or "I wasted years." But blame can hold you back.

- **Acknowledge the Past:** You cannot change what happened.
- **Speak Kindly to Yourself:** Imagine you are comforting a friend who feels guilty. Use that same gentle tone with yourself.
- **Look at Bigger Context:** The marriage might have had problems outside your control. Trying to fix everything alone might not have been possible.

6.12 Reaching Out for Professional Help

Sometimes, friends and family are not enough. A professional counselor, social worker, or psychologist can provide skilled help. They can:

- Teach coping skills for stress or anxiety
- Guide you through unresolved anger or trauma
- Give you tools to rebuild confidence

Therapy can be short-term or longer-term. If cost is a concern, some communities have programs with reduced fees or sliding scales.

6.13 Finding Activities That Bring Comfort

It is easy to get stuck in sadness if all you do is work, care for kids, and worry. Try to find at least one activity that soothes you:

- **Creative Outlets:** Drawing, painting, crafts, or music.
- **Outdoor Time:** Fresh air, a visit to a local park, or gardening if you have space.
- **Social Gatherings:** Low-key meetups with a friend at a coffee place.
- **Learning Something New:** A cooking class or an online tutorial about a fun topic.

These do not have to cost much. The point is to have a break from stress.

6.14 Re-Assessing Personal Values

Sometimes divorce can shake up your sense of self. You might ask, "Who am I without this marriage?" or "What do I stand for now?" Reflection on your personal values can provide direction:

1. **Write Down Values You Respect:** Honesty, kindness, courage, empathy, etc.
2. **Check How You Live Them Day-to-Day:** Are you kind to yourself and others? Do you make time for your health if you say you value well-being?
3. **Adjust Where Needed:** If you say you value friendships, plan small meetups or phone calls.

Living in line with your values can bring deeper satisfaction.

6.15 Handling Unwanted Advice

When you are in a tender emotional state, hearing advice from all sides can be overwhelming. People might say, "You need to date again," or "You should never trust anyone again." This can confuse you.

Strategies:

- Thank them briefly, then decide if it is something you want to follow.
- Filter advice: Ask yourself, "Is this person knowledgeable or are they just reacting?"
- Avoid arguing about it. A simple "I appreciate your concern, I'll think about it" might be enough.

6.16 Engaging with Positive People

Surrounding yourself with those who uplift you can speed your emotional recovery:

- **Identify Draining Personalities:** Some folks only point out your flaws or your ex-spouse's flaws, or they gossip. Limit time with them.
- **Find Encouraging Individuals:** They listen, they offer calm support, and they respect your decisions.
- **Build New Connections:** Join local meetup groups, interest-based clubs, or supportive online forums.

Human connection helps you feel less alone.

6.17 Changing Your Environment

Even small changes in your living space can improve mood. If you had shared decorations that remind you of unhappy times, consider replacing them or putting them away:

- **Rearrange Furniture:** A simple shift can make the space feel new.
- **Add Plants or Soft Lighting:** These can make a place more soothing.
- **Create a Cozy Corner:** A small reading nook or a place to sip tea can provide comfort.

Changing your environment does not have to be expensive. Creativity and small touches can shift how you feel in your home.

6.18 Keeping a Daily Journal

Writing out thoughts can help you understand your feelings. A journal can be private. Jot down:

- How you felt throughout the day
- Any breakthroughs or achievements
- Things you are grateful for

Looking back later, you may see patterns: maybe certain interactions leave you upset, or certain activities boost your mood. This awareness helps you make better choices.

6.19 Humor as Medicine

It might feel strange to laugh during divorce, but humor can release tension:

- **Funny Videos:** Watch short clips that make you chuckle.
- **Comedy Shows:** If you have streaming services or local events, pick a comedian that suits your taste.
- **Silly Moments with Kids or Pets:** A game of pretend with your child or playing fetch with a pet can bring genuine smiles.

Laughter does not cure all problems, but it can relieve stress, even briefly.

6.20 Looking Ahead

Healing does not happen overnight. You may have good days followed by tough days. That is normal. The key is to keep moving step by step. Over time, you can find a renewed sense of self. You might discover new interests or strengths you did not know you had.

6.21 End-of-Chapter Summary

- **Emotional Healing Takes Time:** It is normal to feel grief, anger, and sadness.
- **Practical Routines Help:** Simple routines, check-ins, and limiting negative media can calm your mind.
- **Self-Trust and Closure:** You can find closure on your own if your spouse does not help.
- **Physical Wellness Affects Emotional Health:** Exercise, good sleep, and balanced meals can improve your mood.
- **Avoid Harmful Coping:** Watch for patterns like drinking too much or overspending.
- **Rebuild Self-Esteem:** Focus on small wins, positive self-talk, and supportive friends.
- **Change Your Environment:** Adjust your home, add calming touches, and remove painful reminders.
- **Use Humor and Creativity:** Laughter can help you release tension.
- **Seek Professional Help When Needed:** Therapy or counseling can provide structured support.

In this chapter, we have explored deeper emotional healing. You have learned ways to let go of anger, reframe your thoughts, and care for your mental well-being. In the next sections of this book, we will cover topics like parenting with care, handling social stress, and rethinking future plans. Each step you take to protect your heart will help you build a stable and more peaceful life ahead.

CHAPTER 7

Parenting with Care

When parents decide to separate, the process can be tough on children. They often sense changes in the family, even if they do not fully understand. This chapter will show ways to care for children's emotional needs, maintain stability in their lives, and set a positive tone for how you and your former spouse handle parenting responsibilities. Each child is unique, so you can pick ideas that fit your situation best.

7.1 Telling Your Children About the Split

1. Plan the Conversation in Advance

- If possible, both parents should talk to the children together. This helps them see that, even though you are separating, you can still work as a team for their sake.
- Decide on the main points you want to share, like "Mommy and Daddy are going to live in different places," and "It is not your fault."

2. Keep the Explanation Simple

- If a child is very young, a lengthy explanation might confuse them.
- Use words they know, and be honest but gentle.

3. Reassure Them of Your Love

- Children might fear they will lose one parent or that they caused the split.
- Reassure them that both parents still love them, no matter what.

7.2 Common Emotional Reactions in Children

Children can react differently based on their age, temperament, and understanding of the situation.

1. **Crying and Clinging**: Younger children might become more clingy or cry often.
2. **Anger or Acting Out**: Older children or teens might show anger by defying rules or talking back.
3. **Quiet Withdrawal**: Some kids might go silent and keep their feelings inside.
4. **Questions About the Future**: They might worry about where they will live or if they will have to switch schools.

How to Handle These Responses

- Listen calmly. If a child is crying, hold them gently or let them sit close to you.
- Let them know it is okay to have big feelings and that you understand.
- Keep routines consistent where possible, like mealtime or bedtime, to create a sense of stability.

7.3 Co-Parenting vs. Parallel Parenting

After a divorce, parents might choose different methods of working together:

1. **Co-Parenting**:
    - Both parents talk frequently and try to stay consistent with rules and routines.
    - They may attend important events together, like school programs or medical appointments.
    - Co-parenting requires open communication and a willingness to solve problems peacefully.
2. **Parallel Parenting**:
    - This is used when parents have trouble interacting calmly.
    - Each parent handles tasks in their own household with less direct contact.
    - Schedules are still shared, but communication is kept to the basics and often done in writing (text or email) to reduce conflict.

Choose the option that leads to less stress for the children. If co-parenting discussions always end in arguments, parallel parenting might be safer. Over time, some families move from parallel parenting to co-parenting if relations improve.

7.4 Setting Ground Rules with Your Former Spouse

Even if you do not get along, laying out clear guidelines can help avoid confusion for the kids:

- **Respectful Language**: Do not insult the other parent in front of the children.
- **Shared Calendar**: Use a digital calendar or a shared app to mark pick-up times, drop-offs, and important school events.
- **Decision-Making**: Decide which types of decisions need both parents' input (like medical or educational choices) and which can be made by one parent.

If you have serious disagreements, consider mediation. A neutral mediator can help you both create a parenting plan without going to court again.

7.5 Child Support and Practical Expenses

Child support exists to help cover a child's living costs, including housing, food, clothes, and other expenses. It is important to remember:

- **It Belongs to the Child**: The money is supposed to benefit the child's well-being.
- **There May Be Extra Costs**: School trips, medical bills, or extracurricular activities might not be covered by standard child support.
- **Keep Records**: If you are receiving or paying child support, keep receipts, transaction records, or any communication about changes.

If child support payments do not arrive on time, look into local enforcement agencies or a lawyer's advice. Try to stay calm when discussing money with your former spouse. Anger can escalate and hurt the children's sense of security.

7.6 Staying Involved in Your Children's Lives

In the midst of stress, some parents pull back. But children need to see you care, even if you are busier or dealing with sadness.

1. **Attend Activities**: Go to their sports games, school plays, or parent-teacher meetings. Show them you are still there for them.
2. **Regular Calls and Messages**: If you are not the primary caretaker, call the child or video chat at agreed-upon times. It reassures them that you have not disappeared.
3. **Listen to Their Day**: Ask about their friends, their homework, what they found fun or difficult today. Show real interest.

7.7 Dealing with Mixed Feelings from Children

Children might be angry at one or both parents. They might blame the parent who moved out, or they might blame the parent who asked for the divorce. Here are some tips:

- **Allow Them to Express**: Let them share their sadness or anger. Avoid punishing them immediately for showing negative feelings.
- **Stay Calm**: If they say hurtful words, understand it often comes from pain or confusion.
- **Seek Therapy**: Some families benefit from family counseling to help children express feelings more safely.

7.8 Helping Children Handle Guilt

Kids often blame themselves for the break-up. They might think, "If only I had behaved better, maybe Mom and Dad would stay together." Combat this guilt by:

- **Stressing It Is Not Their Fault**: Repeat as needed. "This decision is between adults and is not because of anything you did."
- **Sharing the Real Reasons (in an Age-Appropriate Way)**: You do not need to give heavy details, but you can say, "We had grown-up problems, and it was not something you could fix."

- **Offering Reassurance**: Let them know they are loved and valued in both households.

7.9 Crafting a Routine for Stability

A schedule helps children feel secure because they know what to expect. If they move between two homes:

- **Use a Calendar**: Hang a simple chart in each home. Mark when they will be at Mom's or Dad's place, special events, and routines.
- **Consistent Bedtimes**: If possible, agree on a similar bedtime in both households.
- **Homework Rules**: Decide how homework will be handled to keep consistency. This might mean a set time each day to do it.

When children know the plan, they feel less anxious. Even older children benefit from knowing what is happening day to day.

7.10 Keeping Boundaries in Adult Conflicts

Children should not be in the middle of adult arguments. If there are unresolved issues between you and your former spouse:

1. **Talk in Private**: Do not argue in front of the kids. If a discussion gets heated, suggest taking a break or moving to a private space.
2. **No Blaming the Other Parent**: Telling a child, "This is all your mom's fault" creates loyalty conflicts. Children often love both parents and do not want to pick sides.
3. **Speak Carefully**: Even if the other parent frustrates you, keep your language calm and neutral around the children.

7.11 Handling New Partners (If or When That Time Comes)

Children can be confused when a parent introduces a new significant other. They might worry they will lose their parent's attention or feel disloyal to the other parent.

- **Go Slow**: Do not introduce every date as a "new parent figure." Wait until you are sure the relationship is stable.
- **Explain in Simple Terms**: "I have a friend I care about. You might see them sometimes, but it does not change my love for you."
- **Respect Feelings**: Children might be shy or resistant. Give them time to adjust. Do not force them to be close right away.

7.12 Special Challenges for Different Ages

1. Babies and Toddlers

- They might not fully understand the concept of divorce, but they sense tension.
- Keep their daily routines (feeding, nap times) as regular as possible.
- Give extra hugs and soothing when possible.

2. Elementary School Kids

- They might ask a lot of "Why?" questions.
- They may worry about practical changes: "Who will take me to school?" "Will I see my friends?"
- Clear, brief explanations help.

3. Preteens and Teenagers

- They might pull away or spend more time with friends.
- They could hide feelings, so check in gently.
- They might resent rules if one household is stricter than the other. Talk openly about why rules exist.

7.13 Supporting Children Through Therapy or Support Groups

1. Individual Counseling

- A child can speak to a therapist about feelings they may not want to share with a parent.
- Therapists can teach coping skills, like how to calm down when upset.

2. Family Therapy

- Sessions include the parent(s) and child(ren).
- It gives everyone a safe place to share feelings with a neutral therapist guiding the conversation.

3. Support Groups for Kids of Divorce

- Some schools or community centers run groups where kids can meet peers who are also dealing with separation at home.
- Sharing experiences can help them feel less alone.

7.14 Discipline and Consistency

When parents are not in the same home, discipline can become confusing for kids if the rules differ a lot. You do not have to match everything exactly, but try to align on major points:

- **Bedtime or Curfew**: If there is a big gap in bedtimes between Mom's house and Dad's house, it can confuse children.
- **Screen Time**: If one house allows unlimited internet use and the other is strict, children might feel stressed or try to manipulate the rules.
- **Chores**: Children should still have age-appropriate tasks like cleaning their rooms or helping set the table, no matter which house they are in.

If you cannot agree on all details, at least talk about the big stuff. Children thrive when they know what is expected of them.

7.15 Staying Alert for Signs of Distress

Children might not say "I'm depressed" or "I'm anxious," but they can show warning signs:

- **Sleep Problems**: Trouble falling asleep, frequent nightmares, or wanting to sleep all day.
- **Loss of Interest**: They stop caring about hobbies or friends they once enjoyed.

- **Frequent Stomachaches or Headaches**: Emotional stress can show up as physical symptoms.
- **Declining Grades**: Grades might drop if they are too anxious or sad to focus.

If you notice these signs, talk gently with the child. Ask if something is bothering them. Consider speaking with a counselor or their teacher to see if they notice changes too.

7.16 Encouraging Open Communication

Children feel safer if they know they can talk to you about good or bad feelings without being judged:

1. **Ask Open-Ended Questions**: Instead of "Are you sad?" say, "How was your day? Anything on your mind?"
2. **Listen Without Interrupting**: Let them finish their thoughts. Avoid jumping in to correct or fix things right away.
3. **Validate Their Feelings**: Say, "I see you're upset. It makes sense you would feel that way."

When children feel heard, they are more likely to share problems sooner.

7.17 School Involvement

Teachers and school staff can be allies:

- **Give a Brief Heads-Up**: Let the teacher know there is a divorce or separation going on so they can watch for behavioral changes.
- **Keep Up with School Events**: Even if you are overwhelmed, try to attend parent-teacher conferences or open houses.
- **Check Homework**: This can be hard if children split time between homes. Develop a system where both parents know about major assignments and tests.

A supportive teacher can help children feel secure and spot issues early.

7.18 Positive Ways to Spend Time Together

Building new memories can help children see that life continues in a stable way:

- **Simple Outings**: A walk in the park, a quick trip for ice cream, or a board game night at home.
- **Creative Projects**: Painting, crafting, or even cooking a fun recipe together.
- **Physical Activities**: Kicking a ball around, riding bikes, or dancing in the living room.

The goal is not to spend a lot of money, but to show consistent presence and care.

7.19 Handling Special Events and Holidays

Holidays and birthdays can be tricky after divorce:

- **Plan Early**: Talk to your former spouse about who will have the child on certain days. If you can, share major holidays or split them in a way that feels balanced.
- **Avoid Competition**: Do not try to outdo the other parent with expensive gifts. Children might feel pressured or confused.
- **Create New Traditions**: If certain traditions are no longer possible, think of new ones. A new cookie recipe on winter holidays or a special birthday breakfast.

7.20 Long-Distance Parenting

If one parent moves far away, staying connected is still possible:

- **Scheduled Video Calls**: Pick times that work for both. A regular schedule helps the child look forward to it.
- **Emails or Letters**: Even in a digital age, children might enjoy getting letters or postcards from a distant parent.

- **Visits**: Plan visits in advance. Make sure travel details are clear so the child can feel secure.

It takes extra effort, but children benefit from keeping bonds with both parents if it is safe and healthy.

7.21 End-of-Chapter Summary

- **Communicating the Separation**: Plan how you will tell your children. Use simple, honest language.
- **Handling Emotional Reactions**: Expect sadness, anger, or withdrawal. Validate their feelings.
- **Co-Parenting or Parallel Parenting**: Choose what works best given your relationship with your former spouse.
- **Child Support and Expenses**: Keep records and remember the money is for the child's well-being.
- **Staying Involved**: Attend school events, keep up with daily routines, and show genuine interest in their lives.
- **Handling Guilt and Blame**: Remind children that the divorce is not their fault.
- **Routines and Boundaries**: Keep schedules consistent and do not bring them into adult conflicts.
- **Dealing with Distress**: Be alert to warning signs. Seek therapy or counseling if needed.
- **Positive Time Together**: Create new traditions and fun memories.
- **Long-Distance Parenting**: Keep communication regular if one parent lives far away.

Children can heal and thrive after a divorce if they feel secure, loved, and understood. Even if your relationship with your former spouse is strained, do your best to protect the kids from conflict and to support their emotional needs. In the next chapter, we will look at how to handle social pressure and community responses, which can also affect children's sense of stability.

CHAPTER 8

Handling Social Stress

Divorce can change your social landscape. Friends, family, and coworkers might have questions or opinions. You might feel awkward in certain social situations or worry about gossip. This chapter explores practical ways to handle these social stresses, from telling your boss at work to attending gatherings where your former spouse might also appear. By learning specific strategies, you can maintain your dignity and feel less stressed about how others react.

8.1 The Social Changes That Come with Divorce

1. Mutual Friends

- You may have built friendships as a couple. Some friends might feel the need to pick sides, or they might drift away.
- Others might remain neutral and supportive to both.

2. Extended Family

- Your former spouse's relatives could have become part of your life. After the split, those relationships may shift.
- Your own relatives might also have opinions or strong reactions.

3. Workplace

- Coworkers might notice changes in your mood or schedule.
- Some may ask personal questions or spread rumors.

These shifts can feel like added stress on top of the divorce itself. Identifying possible social issues ahead of time helps you respond more calmly.

8.2 Telling People About Your Divorce

You do not need to announce your divorce to everyone. However, certain people might need to know:

1. **Close Friends and Family**
   - It is often helpful to tell the people closest to you, so they can support you emotionally.
   - You do not owe every detail. A brief explanation is fine: "We decided to end our marriage. I prefer not to go into details."
2. **Coworkers or Boss**
   - If you need time off for court dates, you may want to let your boss know.
   - Keep the conversation factual: "I am going through a personal change and may need some flexibility for the next few weeks."
3. **Casual Acquaintances**
   - If they ask questions, you can politely say, "Yes, we have separated. I appreciate your concern, but I'm keeping details private."

You have the right to decide how much you share. You do not have to satisfy everyone's curiosity.

8.3 Handling Nosey Questions

Some people might ask, "Why are you divorcing?" or "Whose fault is it?" or "Have you tried counseling?" It can be uncomfortable. Possible responses:

- **Short and Direct**: "This is a personal matter, and I would rather not discuss it."
- **Humor**: "Oh, it's a long story—too long for now!"
- **Redirect**: "I appreciate you asking, but how have you been lately?"

You do not need to defend your decisions to everyone. If someone is too pushy, it is okay to excuse yourself from the conversation.

8.4 Social Events Where Your Former Spouse Might Appear

If you share friends or events (like weddings, birthdays of mutual friends, or community gatherings), you might wonder how to act if you both attend. Tips include:

1. **Plan Ahead**
   - Ask the host if your former spouse is invited. If yes, decide if you feel comfortable attending or if you prefer to skip.
   - If you decide to go, prepare yourself mentally. Consider arriving with a supportive friend to feel less anxious.
2. **Keep Interactions Brief**
   - If you run into your former spouse, a polite greeting might be enough. There is no need to engage in deep conversation.
   - Focus on the purpose of the event (celebrating a friend, etc.).
3. **Avoid Scenes**
   - Keep arguments or tense discussions for private settings. Public scenes can create more gossip and stress for everyone.

8.5 Dealing with Gossip

Unfortunately, gossip often follows a divorce. People may speculate about the reasons or assume details they do not know:

- **When You Hear Gossip**: Resist the urge to confront every rumor. This can feed the drama. Instead, calmly set the record straight if needed and move on.
- **Trusted Allies**: Lean on friends who defend you or gently correct false statements.
- **Don't Fuel the Fire**: If you reveal too many personal details, it may spread quickly. Share with caution.

Remind yourself that gossip usually says more about the gossiper than about you. Over time, people will move on to other topics.

8.6 Changing Your Social Circles

Divorce can sometimes mean losing friends who were closer to your spouse or who do not support your decision. It can be sad, but it also gives you room to build new connections:

1. **Join New Groups**
   - Community classes, volunteer programs, or hobby clubs can introduce you to people with shared interests.
2. **Reconnect with Old Friends**
   - Perhaps you had friends you lost touch with during marriage. Reach out if you think they might welcome you back.
3. **Online Communities**
   - You can find supportive online forums or social media groups for people who share your hobbies or experiences. Just be careful about sharing personal details with strangers.

8.7 Helping Children Handle Social Situations

If you have kids, they might face questions or teasing about the divorce at school or in the neighborhood. Support them by:

- **Role-Playing Responses**: Teach them simple replies, like, "My parents are not living together now, but I'm okay," or "That's private."
- **Encourage Them to Talk**: If someone is teasing them, encourage them to tell you, a teacher, or a trusted adult.
- **Keep Teachers Informed**: Let teachers know about the divorce so they can watch for bullying or changes in behavior.

Children often follow your lead. If they see you handle social stress calmly, they are more likely to do the same.

8.8 Setting Boundaries with Extended Family

1. **Your Own Family**
   - Some relatives may blame you or pressure you to reconcile. Explain kindly that the decision is final and you want to avoid further arguments.
   - If needed, limit contact with family members who cause emotional stress.
2. **Former Spouse's Family**
   - Decide if you want to keep in touch. If you were close to your in-laws, you might still communicate, but only if it is comfortable for both sides.

- If they are negative or stirring trouble, a polite but firm distance might be best.

8.9 Workplace Concerns

Work can be a place of refuge or added stress:

- **Informing Human Resources**: In some workplaces, HR can offer resources like counseling or flexible scheduling.
- **Keeping Personal Matters Private**: You do not have to share every detail with coworkers. A simple "I'm going through a hard time, so please be patient if I seem a bit off" can suffice.
- **Handling Gossip at Work**: If colleagues gossip, focus on your tasks and avoid engaging. If it becomes serious harassment, speak to a manager or HR.

Being professional can help you maintain your reputation and sense of stability during this time.

8.10 Single Social Life: Going Out and Meeting People

After you separate, your social life might shift drastically. You may have more free time if your kids spend weekends with the other parent, or you might feel lonely. Possible steps:

1. **Explore Activities Solo**: Go to events alone if you feel up to it. You might meet new people and discover fresh interests.
2. **Invite a Friend**: If large gatherings feel too overwhelming, start with smaller meetups with a friend or sibling.
3. **Check Local Events**: Museums, libraries, and community centers often host socials or workshops.

Try not to isolate yourself, but also do not rush into the nightlife if you are not ready. Move at your own pace.

8.11 Dealing with Unwanted Flirting or Questions About Your Status

Some people might see you as "available" and start making comments or asking if you want to date:

- **Stay Polite but Clear**: "I'm not looking to date right now. Thank you for understanding."
- **Watch for Pushy Behavior**: If someone keeps pushing, distance yourself or ask for help from a friend if you feel unsafe.
- **No Need to Justify**: You do not have to explain why you are not ready or interested. A short refusal is enough.

8.12 Finding an Emotional Balance in Social Situations

Social events can bring memories of your marriage, or you might feel out of place if others are in couples. Ways to cope:

1. **Have a Support Buddy**
- Bring a friend who knows your situation. They can help steer conversations or give you a reason to leave early if you get upset.
2. **Take Breaks**
- If you feel overwhelmed, step outside for fresh air, or find a quiet corner.
3. **Limit Alcohol**
- Drinking too much can lead to emotional outbursts or regrets. Keep it moderate to maintain control.

8.13 Online Profiles and Social Media

Social media can be a double-edged sword during divorce:

1. **Privacy Settings**
- Review who can see your posts. You might want to set them to "friends only."
- Remove people who stir trouble or spy for your former spouse.
2. **Avoid Emotional Posts**

- Posting complaints about your ex can lead to more stress. It might also be used against you in legal matters.
- Stay aware that screenshots can be taken even if you delete a post.
3. **Respectful Sharing**
- If you want to share that you are divorced, keep it simple. "I'm making some changes in my life," can be enough. Close friends probably already know.

8.14 Social Anxiety and Fear of Judgment

You may worry that people are judging you or that you will run into your former spouse in public. This fear can lead to avoiding social settings:

- **Challenge Negative Thoughts**: Ask yourself if you really know that others are judging, or if it is just worry in your mind.
- **Take Small Steps**: Attend events for a shorter time if needed, then gradually build confidence.
- **Seek Therapy**: If social anxiety is severe, a mental health professional can teach coping techniques.

Most people have their own problems and are not as focused on you as you might fear.

8.15 Forming a New Identity

During marriage, you might have seen yourself as part of a pair. Now, you may feel uncertain about who you are as a single person:

- **Try New Hobbies**: Cooking, painting, dance classes—anything you find interesting.
- **Revisit Old Passions**: Maybe you used to love hiking or writing stories. Explore that again.
- **Surround Yourself with Positive People**: Choose friends who appreciate you and help you grow in healthy ways.

You have the chance to discover parts of yourself that were on hold or overshadowed before.

8.16 Handling Religious or Cultural Expectations

In some cultures, divorce can carry heavy stigma or lead to family disappointment:

- **Supportive Community Leaders**: If your faith community is helpful, talk to a leader about your situation. They might offer guidance or connect you with support groups.
- **Set Boundaries with Judgmental Relatives**: Some relatives may shame you or try to pressure you back into the marriage. You can say, "I respect your views, but this decision is final. Please respect my space."
- **Seek People with Shared Experiences**: Look for others who have gone through divorce in the same cultural or religious setting. They may have advice for handling criticism.

8.17 Hosting Gatherings Yourself

If you fear awkwardness when attending events, consider hosting smaller get-togethers:

- **Invite Supportive Friends**: Having a small group of understanding people can boost your confidence.
- **Keep It Casual**: Potluck dinners, movie nights, or game nights can be low-cost and relaxed.
- **Set Guidelines**: If you are not ready to talk about the divorce, let guests know it is off-limits.

Hosting on your own turf can help you feel in control of the social setting.

8.18 Rebuilding Your Reputation if Damaged

Sometimes a spouse might spread rumors or paint a negative picture of you. If you sense your reputation is hurt:

- **Maintain Good Character**: Stay polite, keep a cool head, and avoid speaking badly about your ex in public.

- **Provide Clarity to Key People**: If someone important (like a close friend, a boss, or a mentor) believes false info, you can gently correct them with facts.
- **Patience**: Over time, people will see how you behave and judge for themselves.

The truth tends to surface, especially if you consistently show responsible, respectful conduct.

8.19 Being Mindful of Your Children's Social Circle (If Applicable)

If you have kids, remember that social changes can affect them too:

- **Playdates**: If your child's friend's parents invite both you and your former spouse, decide if you both can attend peacefully or if it is better for one parent to go.
- **School Events**: Children might not want drama at their school, so respect their space.
- **Communication with Other Parents**: Be polite and keep the focus on the kids, not on personal conflict.

Children pick up on social tension. Working to keep their social life stable can help them cope better.

8.20 Long-Term Social Growth

As time passes, your social life will likely find a new rhythm:

1. **Relationships Change**: Some people will leave your life, while others will become closer. This is natural.
2. **Gratitude for Support**: Show appreciation to friends or family who stood by you. A simple thank-you can strengthen those bonds.
3. **Openness to New People**: As you heal, you might feel more comfortable meeting new folks, potentially including future romantic partners (when and if you decide you are ready).

8.21 End-of-Chapter Summary

- **Social Changes**: Divorce can shift friends, extended family ties, and workplace dynamics.
- **Who to Tell**: You do not owe everyone a detailed explanation, but certain people (like close family or your boss) might need some information.
- **Handling Nosey Questions**: Short, direct answers or polite redirection can keep boundaries intact.
- **Dealing with Shared Social Events**: Plan ahead, keep interactions brief, and avoid public confrontations.
- **Gossip**: Resist feeding rumors. Let your true behavior speak for itself.
- **New Social Circles**: Explore new communities or reconnect with old friends.
- **Workplace**: Maintain professionalism and use HR resources if needed.
- **Online Presence**: Adjust privacy settings and avoid emotional oversharing.
- **Overcoming Anxiety**: Try small steps, find a supportive friend, and consider therapy if needed.
- **Hosting Your Own Events**: A good way to regain control of social interactions.
- **Child's Social Concerns**: Help children navigate questions and teasing by peers.
- **Long-Term Growth**: Over time, you can form a positive new social identity at a pace that suits you.

By staying calm, setting clear boundaries, and choosing who you let into your personal matters, you can reduce social stress. In the chapters ahead, we will look at building self-worth, caring for yourself physically and mentally, and other big topics that arise as you keep moving through and beyond divorce.

CHAPTER 9

Growing Self-Worth

When you go through a divorce, your sense of self-worth can take a big hit. You might doubt your abilities or think poorly of yourself because a major part of your life changed. But self-worth is not decided by a relationship's success or failure. It comes from recognizing your value as a person. This chapter shares ways to grow your self-esteem, feel more confident, and respect who you are as an individual. We will look at practical steps you can use daily. You do not need fancy items or big changes. You can start right where you are.

9.1 Understanding Self-Worth vs. Self-Esteem

These words can be confusing. Some people use them the same way, but there is a small difference:

- **Self-Worth** is the feeling that you matter as a person, no matter what happens in your life.
- **Self-Esteem** is how you feel about your abilities, looks, and overall traits, which can go up or down depending on your circumstances.

For instance, your self-esteem at work might drop if you miss a big deadline. But your self-worth is the deeper knowledge that you are still a valuable human being who deserves respect. Divorce can lower both self-esteem and self-worth if you are not careful. The goal is to keep reminding yourself that your core value does not vanish even if your marriage ends.

9.2 How Divorce Affects Self-Worth

1. **Sense of Failure**
   You might think, "I failed at marriage, so I must be flawed." But that is not accurate. Many factors lead to the end of a marriage, and not all of them are under your control.

2. **Comparisons with Others**
   It is easy to look at couples who appear happy and think, "They can keep a marriage going, but I could not." This comparison can harm your self-esteem. You do not know the full story of anyone else's relationship.
3. **Social Judgments**
   Some communities view divorce negatively, leading you to feel judged or excluded. Outside opinions can make you doubt yourself.
4. **Changes in Roles**
   You might feel lost if you identified strongly as a spouse. Suddenly, that role is gone or changed, and you may ask, "Who am I now?"

All these factors can shake your self-worth. But your true value remains. The aim is to see it clearly again.

9.3 Practical Ways to Build Self-Worth

1. **Check Your Negative Thoughts**
   When a negative thought pops up—such as "I'm not lovable"—try to question it. Ask, "Is this really true, or am I just feeling down right now?" Often, you will find it is just a mood, not a fact.
2. **Set Small Achievable Goals**
   - If you feel you cannot accomplish anything, try setting a small goal. Maybe you will clean out one kitchen drawer or pay a bill on time.
   - When you complete it, notice that you followed through. That small success can remind you that you are capable.
3. **Create a Supportive Environment**
   - Surround yourself with people who see the good in you.
   - Reduce contact (if possible) with those who tear you down or constantly point out your flaws.
4. **Make a "Strengths List"**
   - List qualities you like about yourself (kindness, sense of humor, honesty).
   - Ask trusted friends or family for input. Sometimes they see strengths you overlook.

9.4 Replacing Self-Criticism with Self-Kindness

Many people are harsh critics of themselves. After divorce, you might say, "I'm so stupid for not leaving earlier," or "I must be worthless if my spouse left me." This self-blaming can become a habit. Try switching to self-kindness:

- **Speak to Yourself Like a Friend**
  If a friend went through divorce, you would not call them worthless. You would likely offer support. Practice giving yourself the same gentle words.
- **Correct Yourself Gently**
  If you slip and say something cruel to yourself, correct it. For example, replace "I am a total failure" with "I did my best with what I knew at the time."
- **Stop The Cycle**
  Notice when you fall into negative self-talk. Pause, take a breath, and say a kinder phrase such as, "I am trying, and that is enough right now."

9.5 Building Healthy Boundaries

Sometimes low self-worth leads you to let others walk over you. Good boundaries help you protect your time, energy, and feelings.

1. **Identify Your Limits**
   - How many hours can you spend helping others before you burn out?
   - What topics make you uncomfortable to discuss?
2. **Speak Up**
   - If a person pushes you to do more than you can handle, calmly say, "I would like to help, but I cannot do that right now."
   - If someone pries into your private life, you can reply, "I'm not comfortable talking about that."
3. **Practice Saying No**
   - "No" is a complete sentence. You do not have to justify your reasons if you need to protect your well-being.

Setting boundaries does not make you selfish. It shows you respect yourself and expect others to do the same.

9.6 Affirmations and Why They Can Help

Affirmations are short statements that reinforce positive beliefs. Some find them corny, but research shows repeating certain phrases can slowly change how you see yourself.

- **Examples**
    - "I deserve happiness and respect."
    - "I am learning and growing each day."
    - "My past does not decide my future worth."

Write them on sticky notes or put them in your phone. Look at them daily. It might feel odd at first, but over time, affirmations can become a mental habit that fights negative self-talk.

9.7 Using Your Body Language to Boost Self-Worth

How you carry yourself can affect how you feel inside:

1. **Posture**
    - Stand tall with your shoulders relaxed. This can signal to your mind that you are worth being seen.
2. **Eye Contact**
    - When talking to someone, try to keep comfortable eye contact instead of looking down. It shows self-confidence.
3. **Dress in a Way That Feels Good**
    - You do not need expensive clothes, but wearing something clean, comfortable, and in good condition can improve how you see yourself.

You might not notice instant change, but small details in how you present yourself can make a difference in self-perception.

9.8 Finding Strength in New Activities

Exploring new skills or interests can help rebuild self-worth. When you learn something or enjoy a new hobby, you show yourself you can grow and adapt.

1. **Classes**
   - Consider short community classes in painting, cooking, or other topics that interest you.
2. **Free Online Tutorials**
   - Many platforms offer free lessons on a huge range of subjects.
3. **Local Clubs or Groups**
   - Look for local meetups (like a book club or a fitness group). This can also help you meet new people who share your interests.

The point is to see yourself as more than a divorced person. You are still someone who can learn and enjoy life.

9.9 Giving Back to Others (in a Balanced Way)

Doing good for others can boost self-esteem, but you have to keep it balanced:

- **Volunteer Work**
  - Helping at a local charity or community center can remind you that you have value to share.
  - It also shifts focus away from your worries for a while.
- **Acts of Kindness**
  - Being kind to a neighbor or coworker, offering a small favor, or simply listening to someone can remind you that you make a positive impact.

But be careful not to overextend yourself. You cannot fix everyone's problems or fill every gap. Balance is key.

9.10 Recognizing and Overcoming Shame

Shame is the feeling that you, as a person, are flawed or bad. Divorce can trigger shame if you feel judged by others or if you judge yourself harshly.

- **Identify the Source**
  Where does this shame come from? A critical parent? A cultural belief? A

religious expectation? Recognizing the source can help you see it more clearly.
- **Challenge Unrealistic Standards**
Maybe your family taught you that a "good woman" never divorces. Is that a fair or realistic standard? Times change, and many strong women do divorce for valid reasons.
- **Share Selectively**
Sharing your feelings with a trusted friend or counselor can ease shame. Shame often grows in silence and disappears when we talk to someone who is supportive.

9.11 Leaving the "Victim Mindset"

It is normal to feel like a victim if your spouse hurt you, lied, or caused financial harm. But staying in a victim role can trap you in negative thoughts:

1. **Acknowledge the Pain**
   You cannot heal if you ignore what happened. Admit that it was harmful and caused real hurt.
2. **Focus on Your Power**
   Even if you were wronged, you can choose how you respond now. That might involve legal steps, counseling, or setting boundaries.
3. **Rebuild Your Future**
   Instead of asking, "Why did this happen to me?" ask, "What steps can I take to make my life better now?"

When you see yourself as an active person who can still make choices, your self-worth grows.

9.12 Seeking Help from Professionals

Sometimes, self-worth issues are deep and connected to old experiences (like past traumas or childhood stress). A mental health professional can guide you:

- **Therapists or Counselors**
They can teach methods to handle shame, guilt, or self-criticism in a structured way.

- **Support Groups**
  Being around others who have similar struggles can help you see you are not alone.
- **Coaches**
  Some life coaches focus on self-esteem. Check their credentials to ensure they have proper training.

Reaching out for help is not weakness; it is a sign of taking your own well-being seriously.

9.13 Managing Triggers That Harm Self-Worth

A "trigger" is something that sets off negative feelings or memories. After divorce, triggers might include:

- **Certain Songs** that remind you of your wedding
- **Social Media Posts** showing "perfect couples"
- **Places** where you made shared memories

How to Manage Triggers

- **Limit Exposure**: If seeing certain social media accounts drags you down, unfollow or mute them.
- **Have a Plan**: If you cannot avoid a place (like picking up your child from your old house), prepare yourself mentally. Remind yourself that those memories do not define you now.
- **Replace Bad Memories with Neutral or Positive Activities**: If a certain park makes you sad, try going there with a friend or doing something fun there to create a new association.

9.14 Tracking Progress with a Self-Worth Journal

A self-worth journal helps you see growth over time:

- **Daily or Weekly Entries**
  Write down moments when you felt good about yourself. It could be something small, like you handled a minor conflict at work with patience.

- **Reflect on Challenges**
  If you face a setback, note how you handled it. Even if you did not do it perfectly, you tried.
- **Celebrate Small Wins**
  Instead, acknowledge those wins. Keep them in your journal, so you can see proof that you can move forward and do well.

Over time, these notes can remind you of your strengths when self-doubt creeps in.

9.15 Building Self-Worth in Social Interactions

When self-worth is low, you might avoid social events or worry about what others think. To handle this:

1. **Practice Social Skills**
   - Start small with people you trust. Ask how they are and share a bit about your day.
2. **Speak Up in Groups**
   - If you are in a meeting or group discussion, give your viewpoint. Even if it is brief, it reinforces that your thoughts matter.
3. **Learn to Accept Compliments**
   - Instead of brushing off a compliment, try saying, "Thank you, that means a lot." Over time, you might believe it more.

9.16 Letting Go of Perfectionism

Some women who go through divorce blame themselves for not having the "perfect" marriage. But perfection is not real. Letting go of that idea can help self-worth:

- **Value Effort Over Flawlessness**
  Focus on the fact that you tried, you cared, and you learned.
- **Embrace Mistakes**
  Mistakes are part of being human. You are allowed to make them without losing your value.

- **Realistic Goals**
  If you expect everything in life to go perfectly, you set yourself up for disappointment. Aim for steady improvement instead.

9.17 Seeing Yourself as More Than Your Past

It is easy to let divorce define your entire identity, but you have many other roles:

- **If You Are a Parent**: You are also a guiding figure to your child.
- **If You Work**: You have professional skills, whether big or small.
- **If You Have Hobbies**: You are a painter, a runner, a reader, a craft maker—whatever your interests are.

Keep in mind that you are not just a "divorcee." Recognizing these other parts of who you are can boost your self-worth.

9.18 Taking in Positive Feedback

After a divorce, some people only notice criticism and ignore good things. Make a habit of accepting positive feedback:

1. **Thank People**
   If someone says you handled a situation well, say, "Thanks for noticing. It means a lot."
2. **Write It Down**
   Keep track of positive feedback in your phone or a small notebook. On rough days, review it.
3. **Reflect**
   Ask yourself, "Do I see these good qualities in myself?" Over time, you may recognize them more.

9.19 Sticking to Healthy Routines

Healthy routines can build a sense of stability and show you that you can care for yourself. Examples include:

- **Regular Bedtime**: Getting enough sleep makes you less prone to negative thinking.
- **Physical Activity**: Even a short daily walk can lift your mood.
- **Nutritious Eating**: You do not need a strict diet, but try to include fruits, vegetables, and whole grains.
- **Mindful Breathing**: Taking a few deep breaths when stressed can lower tension quickly.

Seeing yourself keep these routines can remind you that you are capable and worth looking after.

9.20 Being Patient with the Process

Growing self-worth is not instant. There can be days you feel strong and days you feel like you are back at square one. That is normal. Patience is crucial:

1. **Celebrate Improvements**
   Notice even small improvements, such as feeling slightly better about yourself this week than last week.
2. **Learn from Setbacks**
   If something shakes your confidence, think about what you can learn from that moment.
3. **Keep Going**
   Consistency matters. Even if you have a bad day, do not throw away all your efforts. Pick up again when you can.

9.21 End-of-Chapter Summary

- **Divorce Often Lowers Self-Worth**: You might feel like a failure, but divorce does not define your value.
- **Self-Worth vs. Self-Esteem**: Self-worth is your inherent value, and self-esteem relates to how you feel about your skills or traits.
- **Build Self-Worth with Small Steps**: Check negative thoughts, set achievable goals, and list your strengths.
- **Healthy Boundaries**: Saying no and protecting your personal space shows you respect yourself.

- **Affirmations and Body Language**: Simple methods to shift how you see yourself.
- **Use Support**: Friends, family, counselors, or support groups can help you break cycles of shame or low self-confidence.
- **Monitor Triggers**: Limit or reframe things that bring negative feelings.
- **Recognize Your Other Identities**: You are more than just a person who experienced divorce.
- **Long-Term Growth**: Patience is key. Building self-worth is a process that can continue for a lifetime.

In the next chapter, we will look at "Taking Care of You," focusing on how to support your physical and mental health in practical ways. Many of the ideas in this chapter connect with health routines, so combining both can strengthen your overall well-being.

CHAPTER 10

Taking Care of You

When life feels chaotic, self-care is often the first thing to be neglected. You may focus on your job, children, or the legal side of divorce. However, it is crucial to take care of your own health during this period. This chapter will show how to stay on top of your physical and mental well-being without needing fancy equipment or expensive plans. By doing these simple steps, you can reduce stress, handle problems more clearly, and promote better long-term health.

10.1 Why Self-Care Matters More Than Ever

1. **Stress Takes a Physical Toll**
   Ongoing stress from divorce can lead to headaches, muscle tension, stomach issues, or sleep trouble. Caring for your body and mind can lessen these effects.
2. **Better Decision-Making**
   If you are worn out, you might make rash decisions or struggle to keep track of legal tasks. Good self-care helps keep your mind sharp.
3. **Emotional Balance**
   Divorce often includes strong emotions. Keeping your stress level down can help prevent extreme mood swings or burnout.

Many people think of self-care as a luxury, but it is actually a core need, especially during big life changes.

10.2 Physical Health Foundations

1. **Balanced Eating**
   - Try to include fruits, vegetables, lean protein (like eggs, chicken, beans, or fish), and healthy carbs (like whole grains).
   - Limit sugar and processed snacks if you can. These can cause energy crashes.

       - If cooking is tough, consider batch cooking on weekends or using a slow cooker for simple meals.
2. **Regular Movement**
       - It does not have to be a gym membership. A daily walk or at-home stretching can help.
       - Keep it simple: walking 20 minutes a day can boost mood and circulation.
       - If you have specific health issues, check with a doctor before starting a new exercise plan.
3. **Water Intake**
       - Many people do not drink enough water. Aim for around 6 to 8 glasses a day, but adjust if you have certain health conditions.
       - Dehydration can cause fatigue, headaches, and poor focus.

10.3 Guarding Your Sleep

Lack of sleep can worsen stress and hurt your mood. Tips for better rest:

- **Set a Routine**
  Try to sleep and wake at the same time each day, even on weekends if possible.
- **Create a Wind-Down Habit**
  Dim screens and lights an hour before bed. You can read a book (nothing too exciting) or listen to calming sounds.
- **Limit Stimulants**
  Avoid heavy meals, caffeine, or energizing activities close to bedtime.
- **Check Mattress and Pillows**
  A good sleeping surface can reduce back or neck pain that disrupts rest.

If you still cannot sleep well, a doctor or counselor might help. Insomnia often connects to stress or anxiety that needs more targeted care.

10.4 Simple Ways to Lower Daily Stress

1. **Breathing Exercises**
   - One simple method: breathe in for 4 seconds, hold for 4 seconds, breathe out for 4 seconds. Repeat a few times to calm your mind.
2. **Short Breaks**
   - If you work, stand up every hour or two. Stretch or take a quick walk. If you are at home, do the same.
3. **Calm Moments**
   - If you can find even 5 minutes to sit quietly, it can reset stress levels. You might close your eyes and focus on your breath or a relaxing image.
4. **Music or Nature Sounds**
   - Some people feel relaxed listening to calm music or nature sounds while cooking or doing chores.

Try these small tricks throughout the day to manage tension before it piles up.

10.5 Emotional Self-Care

While physical health is key, emotional well-being is just as important:

1. **Journaling**
   - Writing down thoughts or worries can reduce mental clutter.
   - You can also track positive moments to remind yourself of good parts of the day.
2. **Supportive Conversations**
   - Talk with a trusted friend or join a support group.
   - Sharing your feelings can lighten the load, but choose people who are good listeners.
3. **Mindful Activities**
   - Focus on one activity at a time, whether it is washing dishes or sipping tea. Notice the small details to stay grounded in the present.
4. **Practice Self-Forgiveness**
   - Let yourself off the hook for not being "perfect." A small slip in your routine does not erase all your efforts.

10.6 Low-Cost or Free Self-Care Ideas

Self-care does not have to be expensive spa days. Many helpful methods cost little or nothing:

1. **Warm Bath or Shower**
   - Light a modest candle or play soft music. Warm water can soothe tense muscles.
2. **Library Visits**
   - Libraries offer free access to books and sometimes community events or classes. Reading can be a relaxing escape.
3. **Nature Walks**
   - Spending time outside can clear your head. Look at trees, feel the breeze, and note small natural details around you.
4. **DIY Spa Night**
   - Apply a simple face mask (even homemade with oatmeal or honey) and relax for 10 minutes at home.

10.7 Scheduling Regular Check-Ins with Yourself

It is easy to lose track of self-care if you do not make it part of your plan:

1. **Put It on the Calendar**
   - Mark a specific time each day or week for self-care tasks. Treat it like an important appointment.
2. **Ask, "How Am I Doing?"**
   - Once or twice a day, pause and ask yourself how you feel physically and emotionally. Are you hungry, tired, tense? Take small steps to address these needs.
3. **Review Progress**
   - At the end of the week, reflect on what self-care steps worked or did not work. Adjust as needed.

When self-care becomes routine, it is easier to keep doing it, even during stressful times.

10.8 Boundaries Around Your Personal Time

You may feel pulled in many directions after a divorce—children, work, extended family, or even social commitments. Setting boundaries around personal time is vital:

- **Protect Moments of Rest**
  Let others know that you are unavailable at certain times, such as an hour in the evening when you practice relaxing routines.
- **Negotiate Responsibilities**
  If you have older children, ask them to handle small chores so you have a break. If you have a co-parent, make sure tasks are divided in a fair way.
- **Say No When Overloaded**
  If you have too many obligations, it is okay to decline certain invites or tasks. Overextending can harm your health.

10.9 Healthy Social Connections

Humans are social beings, and having supportive connections can be a major part of self-care:

1. **Quality Over Quantity**
   - You do not need 20 friends checking on you daily. A small circle of caring people can be enough.
2. **Buddy System**
   - If you want to improve your fitness, find a walking partner or someone who shares a healthy goal.
3. **Check for Local Groups**
   - Some communities have groups for shared activities like cooking lessons, hiking, or simple gatherings. This can give you a sense of belonging.

Try to avoid people who drain your energy or constantly criticize you. Focus on relationships that bring warmth or understanding.

10.10 Recognizing the Signs of Burnout

Burnout happens when stress builds up too long without relief. Symptoms can include:

- Constant fatigue, even after sleeping
- Irritability or mood swings
- Loss of interest in once-loved activities
- Frequent headaches or physical complaints
- Feeling overwhelmed by small tasks

If you notice these signs, it is time to step back and take more deliberate self-care measures. Talk to a counselor if it feels unmanageable alone.

10.11 Keeping an Eye on Potential Dependencies

When stress is high, some turn to alcohol, food binges, or other habits that can become damaging:

- **Alcohol or Substance Overuse**
  Drinking more than usual to cope might bring short-term relief but risks bigger problems down the line.
- **Excessive Comfort Foods**
  Eating sweets or junk food in large amounts can lead to weight gain and health issues, which can create more stress.
- **Excessive Screen Time**
  Some people watch shows or scroll social media for hours to escape real-life problems. This can increase isolation.

If you see these patterns, seek help. A doctor, counselor, or support group can offer healthier coping tools.

10.12 Creating a Soothing Home Environment

Your home should feel like a safe retreat:

- **Clean and Tidy**
  Clutter can add to stress. Consider a small cleaning routine each day to keep things manageable.
- **Add Personal Touches**
  Photos of loved ones (who make you feel good), a simple plant, or calm colors can lift your mood.
- **Gentle Lighting**
  Use warm lamps or fairy lights instead of harsh overhead lights. This makes evenings more relaxing.

Even if you have a tiny apartment, small changes can make it feel more comforting.

10.13 Short Mindful Techniques

You do not always have an hour to meditate, so shorter techniques can help:

- **30-Second Breather**: Close your eyes, inhale slowly, exhale slowly, and think of one calming word (like "peace" or "calm").
- **Body Scan**: Quickly check how each part of your body feels, from head to toe, and relax tense areas.
- **Name 3 Things You Can See**: If anxiety hits, look around and name three details (for instance, "blue pen," "wooden desk," "green plant"). This brings your focus back to the present moment.

10.14 Seeking Professional Health Check-Ups

When stressed, it is easy to skip doctor or dental visits. However, regular check-ups are important:

1. **Primary Care Appointments**
   - Yearly check-ups can catch issues early. Mention any new symptoms related to stress or lack of sleep.
2. **Mental Health Screenings**
   - If you suspect depression or anxiety, ask your doctor for a screening or referral to a mental health specialist.

3. **Eye and Dental Care**
   - Eye strain or tooth pain can add to overall stress. Keep those appointments if you can.

10.15 Creating a Self-Care Toolkit

A self-care "toolkit" is a set of things you can turn to when you feel overwhelmed. It could include:

- **Breathing or Relaxation Apps**
  Many are free and guide you through short calming exercises.
- **A List of Uplifting Songs**
  Music can shift your mood.
- **Small Treats**
  Items like scented lotions, a cozy blanket, or a puzzle book can give a mental break.
- **Inspiring Quotes**
  Jot them in a notebook or store them in your phone for quick motivation.

Keep these items in an easy-to-reach spot, so you do not have to search for them when stress spikes.

10.16 Handling Cravings for Comfort

Comfort cravings—like a strong desire for chocolate, salty snacks, or even shopping—often arise under stress:

- **Pause and Ask Why**
  Are you genuinely hungry, or is it emotional stress?
- **Healthier Swaps**
  If you want something sweet, maybe fruit or a bit of dark chocolate is enough. If you want to shop, set a small budget for something useful instead of going wild.
- **Alternatives**
  Sometimes, you might just need a break. A short walk or phone call with a friend might reduce the craving.

10.17 Staying Alert to Changes in Mood

Emotional shifts can happen during divorce. Be aware of patterns:

- **Feeling Hopeless**: If you have days where you think nothing will ever improve, that is a sign to seek more help.
- **Sudden Anger**: Intense anger might point to unresolved feelings. Counseling can help you manage them.
- **Tearfulness**: Crying more than usual is not necessarily bad, but if it feels out of control, consider talking to a professional.

It is normal to have mood changes, but when they become intense or unrelenting, added support can be a lifeline.

10.18 Making Time for Simple Pleasures

Self-care also includes moments of small joy:

- **Daily Gratitude**
  Note a few things you appreciate, like a kind neighbor or a tasty meal.
- **Fun Media**
  Watch a movie or a funny video that makes you smile.
- **Engage the Senses**
  Enjoy the warmth of the sun, the sound of birds, or the smell of a good cup of coffee.

These small pleasures build a sense of well-being over time.

10.19 Balancing Alone Time and Social Time

Some people need more alone time to recharge, while others need social contact:

- **Know Your Own Needs**
  Reflect on whether you feel better after time with others or time by yourself.

- **Plan Accordingly**
  If you are drained by large gatherings, choose smaller meetups. If you are lonely, invite a friend for a walk or coffee.
- **Avoid Extremes**
  Do not isolate completely or overschedule yourself. Balance is important.

10.20 Tracking Your Own Care Over Time

To stay consistent, you can keep a simple chart:

- **Date and Activities**
  Write what self-care steps you took each day.
- **Mood Rating**
  Give your day a mood score (like 1 to 10). Over time, see if certain habits link to better moods.
- **Adjust As Needed**
  If a method is not helping, try something else. If a certain method helps a lot, do it more often.

This record helps you see patterns and reminds you that you are working toward better health.

10.21 End-of-Chapter Summary

- **Self-Care Is Not Optional**: Divorce stress makes it more important than ever to care for body and mind.
- **Physical Health Tips**: Balanced eating, daily movement, and enough water can support your health.
- **Sleep and Stress Relief**: Guard your rest and use small tricks to reduce tension, like short breaks or breathing exercises.
- **Emotional Maintenance**: Journaling, mindfulness, and self-forgiveness ease emotional strain.
- **Low-Cost Ideas**: Libraries, nature walks, and simple at-home routines can be as helpful as expensive programs.

- **Protect Your Time**: Set boundaries and schedule self-care in your calendar.
- **Healthy Social Connections**: Choose supportive individuals and avoid people who drain you.
- **Warning Signs**: Watch for burnout or excessive reliance on substances or unhealthy habits.
- **Toolkits and Tracking**: Keep a self-care toolkit on hand and track your progress over time.

When you prioritize your own well-being, you are better able to handle divorce challenges, support loved ones, and plan for a positive future. In the next chapters, we will look at finding new hobbies, rethinking future goals, and other important actions you can take as you progress. Remember: the healthier you feel inside and out, the stronger you become in every aspect of life.

CHAPTER 11

Finding New Hobbies

After a divorce, it can feel like your whole life has changed. You may have extra time on your hands, or you might be looking for healthy ways to stay busy. Hobbies can help fill that gap and bring positive benefits to your day. They are not just for fun, although fun is a key part. They also help reduce stress, boost creativity, and introduce you to people with shared interests. This chapter will explore different kinds of hobbies, show how to pick ones that fit your life, and guide you toward finding simple joy in new activities.

11.1 Why Hobbies Matter After a Major Life Change

When a marriage ends, you might feel sad, worried about the future, or stuck in old routines. A new hobby can help in these ways:

1. **Focus and Calm**
    - When you do something interesting, your mind can get a short break from stress. It is like pressing pause on worries while you concentrate on a pleasant task.
    - Many hobbies allow you to work with your hands or think about one thing at a time, which can help calm the racing thoughts that might come with divorce.
2. **A Fresh Identity**
    - You might have defined yourself mostly as a spouse or caretaker. Now, you can explore another side of yourself that has been quiet for a while.
    - Hobbies let you see yourself as a person with unique interests. This can boost self-esteem because you start to say, "I'm not just someone who went through a divorce; I'm also a painter, a gardener, or a runner."
3. **Balance and Joy**
    - Serious matters like legal documents or financial changes can dominate your days. Having a hobby brings balance, reminding you that life still holds smaller joys.

- Sharing your hobby with friends or family can also build stronger bonds. Sometimes, it creates new connections you did not expect.

11.2 Overcoming Worries About Trying New Things

Many people hesitate to start a new hobby because they fear they will not be good at it or they think it is a waste of time. Here are ways to handle those worries:

1. **Remember It's Not a Contest**
   - A hobby is not about winning awards. It is about relaxing or finding interest in an activity. Even if you are not great at it, you can still get plenty of benefits.
2. **Start Small**
   - If you want to learn painting, you do not need the best brushes or large canvases right away. Begin with simple tools and an online tutorial or a library book.
3. **No Need to Impress Others**
   - This is something you do for your own happiness. Do not worry about negative opinions or whether others think it is useful.
4. **Pick Something That Truly Pulls Your Attention**
   - If you pick a hobby just because you heard it is popular, you might not stick with it. Instead, choose something you feel a real spark for, like baking or dancing.

Overcoming doubt is the first step. You do not have to be an expert. Just let yourself try. If one hobby is not right for you, it is fine to switch to another.

11.3 How to Pick a New Hobby

If you are unsure how to start, consider these steps:

1. **Recall Your Past Interests**
   - Think about what you liked as a child or teenager. Maybe you enjoyed drawing, writing poems, building things, or doing small science projects.

- If you never had a chance to explore those interests before, now might be the time.
2. **Look at Your Current Life**
    - Do you have children? Maybe a hobby you can share with them, like crafting or short nature walks, would be good.
    - Are you busy with work? You might want a hobby that fits into a tight schedule, such as quick 20-minute home workouts or sketching in a small notebook.
3. **Do a Trial Run**
    - If you think you might like yoga, try a free online video or a short community class. If you find it enjoyable, continue. If not, move on to something else.
    - Test-driving hobbies helps you avoid spending too much time or money on something that does not click with you.
4. **Think About Your Comfort Level**
    - If you prefer calm, quiet activities, you might lean toward art, music, or writing. If you like to move, you might pick a sport or dance.

Picking a hobby does not have to be complicated. Just start with simple questions: "What do I like?" and "What fits my life right now?"

11.4 Indoor Hobbies: Creative and Relaxing

If you do not feel like going outside or if the weather is not friendly, many indoor hobbies offer fun and relaxation:

1. **Painting or Drawing**
    - You only need some paper, pencils, and perhaps a small set of paints. You can watch free tutorials online to learn basic techniques. This hobby helps focus the mind and can be very calming.
2. **Knitting or Crochet**
    - Yarn crafts can be soothing, and you can even make simple items like scarves or blankets. Many people find the repetitive motion reduces stress.
3. **Cooking or Baking**

-
  -
    - Trying new recipes can be both practical and fun. You do not have to be a master cook. Start with easy dishes. Over time, you might discover a real passion for preparing meals.
  4. **Reading or Audiobooks**
     - A good book can transport your thoughts to another place. If you find it hard to read because you are busy, try audiobooks during chores or commutes.
  5. **Puzzles and Brain Games**
     - Jigsaw puzzles, crossword puzzles, or Sudoku can sharpen your mind. They can be done alone or with kids and friends.

Indoor hobbies are especially helpful if you prefer a quieter environment or if your schedule only allows small blocks of time.

11.5 Outdoor Activities for Fresh Air

Getting outside can lift your mood and help you stay active:

1. **Walking or Hiking**
   - You do not need special gear for a simple walk. A comfortable pair of shoes and a local park can do wonders. If you feel more confident, you can try easy hiking trails.
2. **Gardening**
   - You can start with a few pots on a windowsill or balcony. Growing herbs or small plants can bring a sense of calm and accomplishment. If you have a yard, planting flowers or veggies can be a bigger project.
3. **Bird Watching**
   - This hobby requires patience and observation. You can download a simple guide or an app to identify local birds. It encourages you to slow down and notice nature's details.
4. **Outdoor Photography**
   - Many smartphones have decent cameras. You do not need a fancy camera to enjoy taking pictures of sunsets, flowers, or cityscapes.
   - Learning composition and lighting can also sharpen your artistic sense.
5. **Local Sports Groups**

- Check if there are beginner-friendly groups for sports like tennis or soccer. You do not have to be a serious athlete. Some communities have casual meetups where people just want to have fun.

Fresh air and sun can help reduce stress and improve your mood. Outdoor hobbies might also provide mild exercise, which is good for health.

11.6 Hobbies That Nurture Creativity

Creativity is not limited to painting or writing. It can show up in many forms:

1. **Music and Singing**
   - If you like music, consider learning a simple instrument like a ukulele. Online tutorials can teach you basic chords. If you prefer singing, you might join a local singing group or practice karaoke at home.
2. **Writing**
   - This can include journaling, short stories, or poetry. Writing helps you process thoughts and can also be a meaningful art form. You do not need to show it to anyone if you do not want to.
3. **Crafts and DIY Projects**
   - This could be making home decorations, refurbishing old furniture, or creating small gifts for friends. The act of making something with your own hands can feel fulfilling.
4. **Handmade Cards and Scrapbooking**
   - If you enjoy memories and design, you can make personalized cards for friends' birthdays or create a scrapbook of meaningful moments. It is a simple way to mix art with memory-keeping.
5. **Upcycling**
   - This is turning old or broken items into something new and useful. It can be fun, creative, and eco-friendly. For example, painting an old wooden box to store supplies or turning empty jars into home organizers.

When you tap into creativity, you may discover hidden talents or simply enjoy the process. It can be a great way to express feelings without words.

11.7 Physical Hobbies That Boost Health

Staying active can help you feel stronger and more confident. If you want a hobby that includes movement, here are some suggestions:

1. **Yoga or Stretch Routines**
   - You can find plenty of beginner videos that teach easy poses. These routines can improve balance, flexibility, and stress relief.
2. **Dancing**
   - Dancing at home or joining a beginner class can lift your mood. Styles can range from hip-hop to country line dancing. Even 10 minutes of dancing can get your heart rate up and put a smile on your face.
3. **Light Weight Training**
   - Simple exercises with light dumbbells or resistance bands can help build muscle. It is often surprising how quickly you can feel stronger by doing a short routine a few times a week.
4. **Swimming**
   - If you have access to a community pool or live near a safe water source, swimming is a low-impact exercise. Many places offer beginner-friendly pool sessions.
5. **Cycling**
   - Riding a bike around your neighborhood or on a bike path can offer good cardio exercise. A basic bicycle and a helmet are all you need to start.

Physical hobbies can help with stress, give you more energy, and improve sleep. Even if you have never been athletic, gentle activities can still offer benefits.

11.8 Social Hobbies for Meeting Others

If you feel lonely after a divorce, hobbies can open doors to new friendships:

1. **Book Clubs**

- Many libraries or community centers host book clubs. You can meet people who like reading, discuss stories, and socialize in a low-pressure setting.
2. **Community Sports or Groups**
    - Some neighborhoods have easy-going sports teams, like a casual softball league or weekend badminton meetups. It is a fun way to exercise and chat with people who share an interest in the sport.
3. **Group Classes**
    - Cooking classes, art workshops, or dance classes often attract people eager to learn in a relaxed environment. Everyone starts out as a beginner, so you do not need to feel out of place.
4. **Volunteer Work**
    - While volunteering is not always called a "hobby," it can fit a similar role. You choose a cause you care about—like an animal shelter or a community garden—and spend regular time there. You may meet like-minded people who share your desire to help.

Joining social hobbies can reduce isolation. It also helps you see that people can appreciate you for who you are now, not just who you were in a marriage.

11.9 Tech-Related Hobbies for Modern Times

If you like gadgets or computers, or if you want to learn new digital skills, consider these options:

1. **Coding or Simple Website Building**
    - You can try free platforms that teach basic coding skills. It can be fun to create small projects or personal sites.
2. **Photography Editing**
    - If you enjoy taking pictures, learn how to edit them with free or low-cost software. Enhancing photos can be a creative outlet.
3. **Online Gaming Groups**
    - Some games allow casual play and include social elements, like chatting with teammates. If you pick games aimed at fun rather than competition, it can be a friendly environment.
4. **Tech Fix-It Projects**

- If you are curious about how things work, you might learn to repair small electronics or computers. You can find step-by-step videos that show you how to fix old gadgets.
5. **Podcasts**
    - Starting your own small podcast can be simple with a microphone and free editing software. You can talk about topics you enjoy or interview local experts.

Tech hobbies can be done at home, often at any time of day. Just be careful not to spend too many hours in front of a screen without breaks, as moderation is still important for health.

11.10 Time Management: Fitting Hobbies Into a Busy Life

You might wonder how to fit a hobby into your schedule if you have kids, a job, or many responsibilities. Here are some ideas:

1. **Start With 15 Minutes a Day**
    - Even a short session can add up over time. Read a few pages in a book, do a quick craft, or practice a musical instrument for just a quarter of an hour.
2. **Use Small Breaks**
    - During your lunch break at work, you could knit a few rows or do a short word puzzle.
    - If you are waiting in a car line to pick up kids, you could plan your next cooking experiment or do a quick language lesson on a phone app.
3. **Block Out Hobby Time**
    - Look at your weekly schedule and block out a dedicated slot. For example, Saturday mornings from 9 to 10 might be your painting hour.
4. **Combine Hobbies with Existing Tasks**
    - If you have to cook dinner, maybe turn it into a cooking hobby session. Try a new recipe or technique each night.
    - If you need exercise, join a local walking group so it becomes both a social and physical hobby.

Remember that hobbies do not have to take huge chunks of time. Small steps can bring big rewards.

11.11 Budget Concerns: Finding Affordable Hobbies

Some hobbies can be costly, but there are many budget-friendly ways to explore new pastimes:

1. **Use the Library**
   - Libraries often lend not only books, but also movies, music, and sometimes tools or art supplies. They may also have free classes.
2. **Secondhand Stores**
   - You can find art supplies, sports equipment, and many other items at thrift shops for a fraction of the cost.
3. **Borrow Before Buying**
   - Ask friends if you can borrow a camera, guitar, or other item to see if you truly like a hobby before purchasing your own.
4. **Free Online Tutorials**
   - There are countless videos and articles that teach you everything from painting to coding without charging you.
5. **Nature and Public Spaces**
   - Parks and beaches are free for walking, photography, picnics, or simply relaxing.

The main cost for many hobbies is time, not money. A bit of planning can keep you from overspending and help you enjoy activities without financial stress.

11.12 Building Confidence Through Hobbies

One great hidden benefit of hobbies is how they can strengthen your sense of self:

1. **Achievement and Progress**
   - When you learn even a small skill, like playing a simple tune on a piano or growing your first tomato plant, you realize you can achieve things on your own. This feeling builds self-worth.

2. **Social Support**
    - If you join a group class, people often encourage each other. Hearing a kind word from a classmate or teacher helps you see yourself more positively.
3. **Healthy Distraction from Worries**
    - Focusing on a creative or active task can interrupt negative thoughts. You may notice that your mind feels clearer after practicing a hobby.
4. **Goal-Setting**
    - You might set a small goal, such as finishing a short story or being able to jog a certain distance. Reaching that goal can show you that you have the ability to plan and succeed.
5. **Learning to Accept Imperfections**
    - Mistakes happen in any hobby. You might drop a stitch while knitting or miss a note while singing. Over time, you learn that mistakes are part of the process. This attitude can carry over into other parts of life, making you more forgiving toward yourself.

11.13 Avoiding Stress: Tips for Making Hobbies Work for You

Sometimes a hobby can become stressful if you put too much pressure on yourself. Avoid that trap:

1. **Keep It Light**
    - If you start feeling like you must practice every single day or reach certain levels fast, you might lose the fun. Let it be a nice break from daily stress.
2. **Do Not Compete Unless You Want To**
    - Some people enjoy competitions (like local art shows or 5K races). Others get stressed by it. Know your own comfort level.
3. **Stay Flexible**
    - Your hobby schedule might change if you have a busy week. That is normal. You can pick it up again when time allows.
4. **Try New Angles**
    - If you feel bored with your hobby, do not give up. Maybe switch from watercolor to acrylics, or from classical guitar to learning pop songs. Minor changes can bring back excitement.

5. **Avoid Comparing**
   - Seeing someone else's advanced skills can make you feel behind. But they might have been practicing for years. Focus on your own progress, no matter how small.

Hobbies should reduce stress, not create more. If you ever feel pressure, take a step back and remember the original reason you started: to relax and enjoy yourself.

11.14 Final Thoughts on Finding New Hobbies

Taking up new hobbies after a divorce can be a strong step toward a healthier and happier life. It is a way to reconnect with yourself and discover parts of your personality that might have been quiet for a long time. Whether you choose an indoor pursuit like painting or an outdoor activity like gardening, each moment spent doing something you enjoy can raise your spirits.

- **You Are Allowed to Explore**: There is no single "right" hobby. Pick what you like, and do not be afraid to switch if it is not working.
- **Keep it Manageable**: Fit it into your budget and schedule so it feels like a joy instead of a burden.
- **Share Your Hobby If You Wish**: Sometimes doing a hobby with a friend, child, or new acquaintance can brighten the experience.
- **Track Your Feelings**: Notice if your stress goes down or if you feel more excited about the week because of your hobby time.

A divorce can bring sadness or confusion, but it can also open doors. Hobbies are one door to new knowledge, creativity, and friendships. By trying something that sparks your interest, you show yourself that you still have many things to look forward to in life. You may even find a talent you never knew you had. With this in mind, you can step confidently into activities that bring a sense of progress and fulfillment.

CHAPTER 12

Re-thinking Future Plans

After a divorce, it can feel like the entire map of your life has been redrawn. Perhaps you had long-term goals together with your spouse—like owning a house, traveling somewhere special, or raising children in a certain way. Now, you may wonder how to adjust those dreams or create new ones. This chapter explores practical methods to think about the future, set new goals, and handle any fear or excitement that comes with them. Re-thinking future plans is not about discarding everything you once wanted; it is about shaping a path that fits who you are now.

12.1 The Importance of Looking Ahead

1. **Why Plan at All?**
   - Some people feel overwhelmed and want to take life day by day. While short-term thinking can help in times of extreme stress, having a vision can also give direction and motivation.
2. **Emotional Benefit**
   - When you imagine better days ahead, you may feel hope. This is especially true if you outline specific steps to get there, rather than just vague wishes.
3. **Practical Benefit**
   - Having goals related to finances, career, or personal growth can help you focus energy on the right tasks. You can reduce the chance of feeling lost because you have a roadmap, even if it changes along the way.

Looking ahead does not mean ignoring the present. Rather, it means setting a course you can work toward, one step at a time.

12.2 Understanding the Shift in Your Priorities

Your priorities might be different now compared to when you were married:

1. **Personal Freedom**
   - Maybe you want more freedom to travel or live in a different place. Or perhaps you want to develop your own business without worrying about a partner's approval.
2. **Family Responsibilities**
   - If you have children, they are still a priority. But the way you raise them, budget for them, or plan their future might shift with only one parent in the household, or with co-parenting schedules.
3. **Career and Money Goals**
   - Perhaps you had been leaning on a spouse's income, or you had put your career on hold. Now you might want to step forward to improve your financial security.
4. **Emotional Well-Being**
   - Protecting your mental health may become a bigger goal. This might lead you to reduce extra burdens or step away from stressful environments.

It is normal for your values and focus to change. The key is to recognize what truly matters to you in this new phase.

12.3 Setting Goals That Fit Your New Life

1. **Short-Term vs. Long-Term Goals**
   - Short-term: Actions you can take in the next few weeks or months, like updating your resume or re-organizing your home.
   - Long-term: Bigger plans for the next few years, such as finishing a degree, buying a home on your own, or moving to a new location.
2. **Making Goals Realistic**
   - If you aim too high right away, you might get discouraged. For example, if you have financial struggles, setting a goal to save a huge amount in a short time may add stress. Instead, start with small steps.
3. **Breaking Down Each Goal**
   - If your long-term goal is to get a better job, your short-term steps might be: polish your resume, look at job listings twice a week, apply to one or two positions each week, and perhaps take an online course to upgrade a skill.

4. **Regular Review**
    - Life keeps changing, especially after a divorce. Check on your goals every month or two. If you see something is not working or your priorities have shifted, adjust them without feeling guilty.

Setting goals that fit your reality can give you direction and control in a time when you might feel uncertain.

12.4 Handling Fear of the Unknown

Planning for the future can also bring anxiety because nothing is guaranteed. You might worry about failing at new ventures or not having enough money. Consider these points:

1. **Accept Some Uncertainty**
    - Life rarely goes exactly as planned. Recognizing this can reduce the shock if changes happen.
2. **Focus on What You Can Control**
    - You cannot fully control the job market, but you can keep learning new skills. You cannot control someone else's actions, but you can control your own choices.
3. **Make a Backup Plan**
    - If you are worried about finances, set aside a small emergency fund. If you fear a new job path might not work, keep a simpler path in mind.
4. **Seek Support**
    - Talk to a counselor or a trusted friend about your worries. Sometimes speaking about your fear makes it feel smaller and easier to handle.

Fear often loses power when you take steps. Each small action can calm the mind because you see that you are doing something constructive.

12.5 Re-thinking Your Home Situation

Many people's living arrangements change after divorce. Perhaps you cannot afford the old house on your own, or you want a place with fewer memories. Some thoughts on planning a new home setup:

1. **Renting vs. Buying**
    - If finances are tight or uncertain, renting can be a smart short-term solution. You might wait until your income is stable before buying.
2. **Location**
    - Do you want to be closer to your job or your child's school? Do you want a fresh start in a new city? Weigh the pros and cons of moving far away from your support network.
3. **Downsizing**
    - A smaller home can be cheaper and easier to maintain, giving you more funds for other goals. It can also reduce stress if you do not need so much upkeep.
4. **Making a House Feel Like Home**
    - Even if you rent a small place, you can decorate it in ways that lift your mood, like adding pictures you love or painting a wall in a soothing color.

Moving is a big decision. Take time to explore options and run the numbers. Think about how each choice aligns with your long-term plans.

12.6 Adjusting Career and Education Paths

Another aspect of future planning involves work or further learning:

1. **Exploring New Careers**
    - If you had to abandon a dream job because of marital obligations, this might be your chance to revisit that dream. Research the field, check required skills, and do an honest assessment of your strengths.
2. **Going Back to School**

- 3. **Asking for Help**
    - Some organizations offer grants or scholarships for adults returning to education, especially single parents. Seek out resources through local community centers or official websites.
- 4. **Balancing Work and Family**
    - If you have kids, you need to see what child care solutions are possible. Maybe a family member can help, or you can arrange child care that aligns with your class or work schedule.

        - Adult learners attend college or vocational programs more often these days. Look for night classes, weekend courses, or online programs that fit your schedule.

Upgrading your career or pursuing education can bring new prospects and increase your financial stability. It may take time, but each class or step is an investment in your future.

12.7 Financial Planning for a Stronger Future

Finances can be one of the toughest parts after divorce. Thinking about future money plans is crucial:

1. **Monthly Budget**
    - Make a clear budget that shows income and expenses. See where you can save, even if it is a small amount.
2. **Debt Management**
    - If you have debts, look into repayment strategies. Sometimes, contacting creditors for lower interest rates or consolidating debt might help.
3. **Emergency Fund**
    - Even a small amount set aside each paycheck can protect you from sudden problems like car repairs or medical bills.
4. **Long-Term Savings**
    - Over time, you might grow an account for a down payment on a home, your children's education, or your retirement.
    - If you have access to a retirement plan at work, consider contributing something regularly.
5. **Seek Expert Advice**

- If finances are confusing, try to find a financial counselor or online resources that guide you. They can help you set realistic goals and avoid common pitfalls.

Strong financial planning can reduce stress and help you feel more confident about your independence.

12.8 Raising Children with New Plans

If you have children, your future plans often revolve around their well-being:

1. **Talk to Them About Changes**
   - Children worry about moves, school changes, or whether they can still do certain activities they like. Explain things simply, so they are not left guessing.
2. **Include Them in Simple Decisions**
   - If you are planning to move, you can ask their opinions on room colors or fun ways to arrange furniture. This helps them feel included.
3. **Set Their Routines**
   - Even if your overall life is changing, keeping consistent bedtimes, family meals, or weekend activities can add stability for kids.
4. **Plan for Their Future**
   - Look into education savings plans, or if that is not possible right now, plan how you might help them with career ideas or smaller savings when they are older.

Children sense more peace if they know you have a basic plan for them. It does not have to be perfect, but it helps them trust that life will be okay.

12.9 Building New Friendships and Connections

Future planning is not just about finances and career. It also involves the people in your life:

1. **Quality Connections**

- You might be open to forming friendships with those who share your values. This can happen through community events, volunteering, or even online groups.
2. **Allowing Yourself to Trust Again**
    - If you faced betrayal in your marriage, trusting new people might be tough. It is okay to take small steps. You do not have to rush into deep friendships or relationships.
3. **Define Boundaries**
    - If you meet someone new, whether a friend or a potential partner, think about what kind of relationship you want. Keeping healthy boundaries can prevent repeating old patterns.
4. **Support Systems**
    - A good circle of friends or loved ones can make future planning less scary. They might offer advice or simply cheer you on when you reach a milestone.

Think about how you want your social life to look. Strong connections can make the path ahead feel less lonely.

12.10 Deciding If or When to Date Again

Some people want to remain single for a while; others feel ready to date sooner. Either choice is okay. Here are points to consider:

1. **Emotional Readiness**
    - Ask yourself if you have processed the divorce and are not carrying heavy bitterness. Jumping into dating just to avoid being alone might lead to more pain.
2. **Boundaries in Dating**
    - Think about what you will accept or not accept in a partner. It helps to have clear standards so you do not settle for an unhealthy relationship.
3. **Being Clear About Your Needs**
    - If you have children, you need someone who understands that you are a parent first. If you have career goals, you need someone who respects your ambitions.
4. **Where to Meet People**

- Some prefer online dating sites. Others might meet through hobbies, friends, or social events. There is no single right method, but safety is key. Be cautious, and if you have children, introduce a new person only when you feel very sure.

Dating is a personal decision. If you decide to do it, go step by step. If not, you can still have a fulfilling life on your own while focusing on other plans.

12.11 Emotional and Mental Health as Part of Future Plans

Keeping a healthy mind is part of building a better future:

1. **Ongoing Therapy or Counseling**
   - Some people find that continued sessions, even once a month, can help process new worries or handle stress.
2. **Healthy Coping Skills**
   - You have learned ways to handle stress—maybe journaling, exercise, or breathing exercises. Keep these tools as part of your regular life.
3. **Check for Lingering Anger or Regret**
   - If you find you are still very angry at your former spouse or at yourself, talk it out or seek guidance. Lingering anger can slow your progress.
4. **Reward Your Progress**
   - If you reach a milestone, such as finishing a course or paying off a debt, allow yourself a small reward or a quiet pat on the back. This helps you see the value in your efforts.

Emotional wellness supports every other plan you set. Think of it as the foundation on which you build your next steps.

12.12 Staying Flexible and Open to Change

Even the best plans can shift. Life events like a job offer, a health concern, or changing family needs can alter your path:

1. **Have a Plan, But Stay Adaptable**
    - Write down your goals, but do not see them as strict rules. They are a guide. If a big change happens, you can adjust rather than feeling like you failed.
2. **Look for Good Surprises**
    - Sometimes, unexpected events can open new doors. Maybe you lose a job but discover a better opportunity. If you remain open, you might find paths you did not consider.
3. **Avoid Perfectionism**
    - You do not have to create the perfect future. You only need a direction that feels healthy and right. Small missteps do not ruin everything.
4. **Focus on Learning**
    - Each new situation can teach you something about yourself or the world. Over time, you gather knowledge that helps you make even better plans.

Being flexible means you do not break under sudden pressure. You bend, adjust, and continue moving forward.

12.13 Realistic Timelines for Your Goals

People often underestimate how long it takes to rebuild. Here is a rough idea:

1. **Immediate Phase (Months 1-6)**
    - You might still be dealing with legal matters, figuring out finances, and handling day-to-day emotional swings. Your plans might be small: create a basic budget, find a new place to live, and ensure children are stable if you have them.
2. **Mid-Term Phase (Months 6-24)**
    - You could be taking steps to improve your work situation, or you might be settling into a new home. Perhaps you begin a new class or pay off certain debts. Your emotional recovery might be more steady by now, allowing you to think bigger.
3. **Long-Term Phase (2 Years and Beyond)**

- Here, you might aim for higher career goals, a major move, or deeper personal changes like training for a marathon or finishing a degree program.

Everyone's timeline is different. Some recover faster, and some need more time. The key is to recognize it is a process. You do not have to rush.

12.14 Surprising Facts and Tips for Future Success

- **Small Wins Add Up**: Accomplishing one small goal, like learning a new software tool, can pave the way for bigger career moves.
- **Networking Matters**: Whether it is in-person or online, knowing people can lead to new work opportunities, resource sharing, or emotional support.
- **Self-Care Never Stops**: Even years after divorce, keep your self-care routines strong. This keeps your mind and body ready for life's ups and downs.
- **Children Adjust in Time**: Studies show that children often adapt when a parent finds stable new paths. They like to see you thriving, so do not feel guilty about having personal goals.
- **You Might Inspire Others**: When friends or family see you making positive changes, they might feel motivated in their own lives.

These facts show that rebuilding your future can have a bigger impact than you realize, possibly touching others' lives as well.

12.15 Putting It All Together

Re-thinking future plans is like creating a personal roadmap for the next part of your life:

1. **Look Inward**
   - Ask yourself what you value most: is it security, creativity, raising children well, or personal freedom? Arrange your plans around these core values.
2. **Write It Down**

- Use a journal, a planner, or a digital note to list short-term and long-term goals. Keep track of progress and feelings.
3. **Share with Trusted Allies**
    - If you have a close friend, sibling, or counselor, talk about your plans. They can offer suggestions or keep you accountable.
4. **Stay Flexible but Determined**
    - Life changes happen. Adjust if you must, but do not lose sight of the bigger picture.
5. **Celebrate Milestones**
    - Acknowledge each achievement. For example, if you manage to save a certain amount of money or finish a new skill course, give yourself a small treat or share the news with a friend.

Future planning after divorce is not about forgetting the past. It is about allowing yourself the chance to shape a new chapter on your own terms. You gain control, step by step, as you outline goals that suit your changing life. Whether you dream of a more stable home, a more rewarding career, or simply more peace in your daily routine, you can move toward that reality with consistent effort.

12.16 End-of-Chapter Summary

- **Looking Ahead**: Planning brings hope and direction, even if you still feel overwhelmed.
- **Shift in Priorities**: Your goals may be different now. Acknowledge what truly matters to you as an individual.
- **Goal-Setting**: Break goals into short-term and long-term steps. Review them often and adjust as needed.
- **Handling Fear**: Some uncertainty is normal. Focus on what you can control and consider backup plans.
- **New Home and Work Paths**: Think about renting vs. buying, job changes, and possible training or education.
- **Financial Plans**: Create a budget, manage debt, build an emergency fund, and seek expert advice if you can.
- **Children's Needs**: If you have kids, reassure them and keep them informed about changes that affect their lives.
- **Social and Emotional Growth**: Build new friendships, decide if or when you want to date, and continue caring for your emotional health.

- **Flexibility**: Life will throw surprises. Adapt while keeping your core values in mind.
- **Realistic Timelines**: Rebuilding life can take months or years. Small steps each day lead to bigger change.

By reconsidering your plans in a thoughtful way, you open the door to a life that better reflects your needs and desires. You show yourself that divorce does not end your hopes for the future. It can be the moment you find stronger, clearer direction. Even if you start with one small goal—like taking a class or saving a little each month—you are already moving forward. Over time, these small steps add up to a future that feels steady and fulfilling.

CHAPTER 13

Navigating Court

Divorce can move from calm discussions to a formal court setting. You may have tried to solve issues with your spouse on your own or through mediation. But if you cannot reach an agreement, you might find yourself in a courtroom before a judge. This chapter explains how to handle the court process in a simple, clear way. It also covers how to manage anxiety, prepare evidence, and conduct yourself so you can feel more at ease in a place that often feels intimidating.

13.1 Understanding the Court Setting

1. **Who Will Be There?**
    - **Judge**: The person who makes final decisions if both sides cannot agree. The judge keeps order, listens to each side, and decides based on the law.
    - **Bailiff or Court Officer**: Maintains safety and order, helps the judge with procedural matters.
    - **Court Clerk**: Handles paperwork and organizes documents.
    - **Attorneys**: If you and your spouse each have a lawyer, they will speak on your behalf.
    - **Witnesses**: In some cases, friends, relatives, or experts (like a counselor or financial expert) might testify.
    - **You and Your Spouse**: You both have the right to attend and speak (or have your lawyer speak for you).
2. **What the Room Looks Like**
    - The judge usually sits at a raised desk at the front.
    - Attorneys or individuals (if they do not have attorneys) usually stand or sit at separate tables.
    - There may be a seating area for observers.
    - It is formal: you typically address the judge as "Your Honor," and you must speak only when permitted.
3. **Why Court Might Be Required**
    - If you and your spouse cannot agree on key issues like child custody, property division, or spousal support, a judge must settle it.

- If one side does not follow prior agreements, the other might ask the court to enforce orders.

Knowing the layout and who is involved can reduce some fear. You will see that, while court is serious, it follows a structured process.

13.2 Steps Before the Hearing

1. **Paperwork**
    - You or your lawyer will file motions or documents explaining what you seek (like a certain child custody plan or property split).
    - The other side might file responses. These papers set the stage for what the judge will review.
2. **Gathering Evidence**
    - Collect records: bank statements, emails, texts, photos, or anything relevant to the disagreement.
    - Make sure you label and organize them clearly. If a lawyer is helping, they will guide you on how to present this evidence.
3. **Witness Preparation**
    - If you have witnesses (like a neighbor who saw certain behavior or a teacher who can speak about your child's needs), confirm they can attend.
    - Inform your lawyer about what each witness will say so there are no surprises.
4. **Dress and Etiquette**
    - Although you do not need expensive clothing, choose neat, modest attire. A collared shirt, simple blouse, or plain pants are usually acceptable.
    - Wear shoes that are not too casual. Avoid loud accessories or items that draw too much attention.
5. **Plan Your Arrival**
    - Find out where the courthouse is, how to get there, and where to park.
    - Leave early to account for traffic or security lines at the entrance.
    - Bring the necessary identification and copies of your court papers.

Good organization can reduce last-minute panic. Make a checklist if it helps: documents, directions, and time schedule.

13.3 Courtroom Behavior

1. **Entering and Waiting**
   - Once you arrive, you will likely sit in a waiting area or inside the courtroom until your case is called.
   - Stay calm. You may see other people waiting for different cases.
2. **Addressing the Judge**
   - Stand when the judge enters or when you speak.
   - Speak clearly and politely. If the judge asks you a question, answer directly, without rambling.
   - Do not interrupt the judge or your spouse's lawyer when they are talking. If you strongly disagree, note it down and address it when it is your turn.
3. **Handling Questions**
   - You or your lawyer might present your side first or second, depending on the situation.
   - Answer questions honestly. If you do not know something, say "I don't know."
   - If a lawyer asks you a tricky question, pause and think. Give a short, truthful answer.
4. **Showing Respect**
   - Even if your spouse or their lawyer says something that angers you, do not shout or use rude language. That behavior can harm your credibility.
   - Remain calm, take a breath, and respond when it is appropriate.

Your attitude in court matters a lot. Judges often pay attention not just to what you say, but how you act.

13.4 Presenting Your Evidence

1. **Relevance**
   - The judge only wants information related to the issues at hand. If you bring up unrelated points, the judge might ignore them.
   - For example, if you are discussing child custody, focus on parenting duties, stability, and the child's well-being.
2. **Organization**

- Keep documents in folders, labeled by category (bank records, text messages, receipts).
- If you are representing yourself, the court might ask for copies. Be sure you have enough copies for the judge, the other side, and yourself.

3. **Telling Your Story**
    - Evidence can include:
        - Pay stubs to show income.
        - Lease or mortgage statements to show living costs.
        - Text messages that show attempts at cooperation or details about conflicts.
    - If needed, highlight your main points: "Here is a text where I tried to schedule visits for our child, and my spouse did not respond."

4. **Witness Testimony**
    - If witnesses speak for you, they will be sworn in. They must tell the truth.
    - The judge or your spouse's lawyer may ask them questions (cross-examination).
    - Prepare your witnesses by telling them to stay calm, answer only what is asked, and not to volunteer extra details that could confuse the issue.

Clarity is key. You want the judge to see exactly why your position is reasonable. The less you ramble, the easier it is for the court to follow.

13.5 Cross-Examination and How to Respond

Cross-examination is when the other side's lawyer (or your spouse, if they do not have a lawyer) questions you or your witness. It can feel tense, but here are tips:

1. **Stay Polite**
    - Do not argue with the questioner. Even if they seem pushy or accusatory, stay composed.
    - If a question is unclear, politely say, "I'm sorry, I don't understand the question."
2. **Answer Briefly**
    - Yes/no answers are often enough unless you need to explain.

- If the lawyer tries to make you say something that is not true, calmly correct them: "That is not correct" or "I need to clarify."
3. **Avoid Guessing**
    - If you do not remember, say so. Guessing under pressure can hurt your case if you turn out to be wrong.
    - Sticking to facts helps you keep credibility.
4. **Manage Your Nerves**
    - It is normal to feel upset if the other side is suggesting you did something you did not do. Breathe, think, and respond with facts.
    - You can keep eye contact with the judge instead of staring at the other lawyer if that helps you stay calmer.

Cross-examination can feel like an attack, but it is simply part of the process. Calm, honest answers usually work best.

13.6 Possible Outcomes

After both sides present evidence and witness statements, the judge might:

1. **Make an Immediate Ruling**
    - In simpler cases, the judge might decide right away on matters like property division or spousal support.
2. **Take Time to Decide**
    - In complicated cases, the judge might want to review documents more carefully. The ruling could come days or weeks later.
3. **Order Further Actions**
    - The judge might order a mediator, request more documents, or schedule another hearing if something is unclear.

Remember, the judge's role is to follow the law, consider fairness, and do what seems best for any children involved. Even if the ruling is not what you hoped, keep your composure. You may have options to file an appeal or request changes later if circumstances shift.

13.7 Dealing with Unwanted Outcomes

Sometimes, the judge's decision feels unfair. If you face a ruling you did not want:

1. **Ask Your Lawyer About Next Steps**
    - There may be grounds to appeal or request a modification in the future. However, appeals can be expensive and time-consuming.
    - If you do not have a lawyer, you can still consult one briefly to see if it is worth appealing.
2. **Follow the Orders**
    - Even if you plan to challenge the ruling, follow the judge's orders unless your lawyer advises otherwise. Ignoring them can lead to legal trouble.
3. **Emotional Impact**
    - It is normal to feel upset or frustrated. Talk to a friend or counselor. Taking out anger on your spouse or the court system can create more problems.
4. **Plan for the Future**
    - If you cannot change the ruling immediately, think about how you will adapt. For instance, if child support is less than you wanted, you might need to adjust your budget or look for more income sources.

Sometimes, a less favorable decision can be temporary. If you keep solid records and circumstances change, you can return to court. Judges often allow modifications to child custody or support if a parent's situation shifts.

13.8 Handling Threats or Intimidation

In rare cases, a spouse might threaten you to sway your court approach. They may:

- Threaten to make false claims.
- Pressure you not to show up to court.
- Harass or stalk you.

Steps to Protect Yourself

1. **Document Everything**
    - Save texts, voicemails, or emails that show threats.
    - If it happens in person, jot down the date, time, and words used.
2. **Contact Authorities**
    - If the threats are severe or you fear physical harm, call the police.
    - You might seek a restraining order if you believe you are in danger.
3. **Inform the Court**
    - Let your lawyer (or the judge if you do not have a lawyer) know about any intimidation attempts.
    - Courts take such actions seriously and may offer extra security measures.

Your safety is the top priority. Never ignore serious threats. Many courts provide support or direct you to local services for protection.

13.9 Representing Yourself (Pro Se)

If you cannot afford a lawyer, you might represent yourself:

1. **Study the Rules**
    - Court procedures can be found on websites or in local libraries. Some courts offer free info sessions for self-represented people.
    - Learn how to file documents and handle evidence.
2. **Stay Organized**
    - Keep all your documents labeled. Arrive with copies for all parties.
    - Practice a clear, concise statement of what you want and why.
3. **Ask Court Staff (Within Limits)**
    - The clerk can explain forms or direct you to resources, but they cannot give legal advice.
    - Look for legal aid groups or free clinics if you need more help.
4. **Watch Court Videos**
    - Some courts post videos explaining the divorce process. Watching them can give you a preview of what to expect.

Representing yourself can be challenging, but many people do it successfully by being prepared, polite, and thorough.

13.10 Tips for Testifying with Confidence

1. **Practice**
   - Before the hearing, say your main points out loud to a friend or even to yourself in a mirror. This helps you feel more comfortable speaking in front of others.
2. **Pace Yourself**
   - Speak slowly and clearly. Rushed words can sound nervous.
   - If you lose your train of thought, take a breath and pick up where you left off.
3. **Stick to Facts**
   - Avoid exaggerations or opinions that cannot be proven. Judges rely on facts, not drama.
   - If you are asked about your feelings, be honest, but do not let emotions run wild.
4. **Body Language**
   - Stand or sit up straight, keep hands still or folded calmly.
   - Look at the judge when speaking. Keep calm eye contact.

Confidence does not mean aggression. It means showing that you believe in your statements and have organized thoughts.

13.11 Negotiations in the Courthouse Hallway

Sometimes, right before or between court sessions, lawyers or spouses will talk in the hallway to see if a last-minute agreement can be reached:

1. **Advantages**
   - If you agree on some issues, you can reduce the time in front of the judge. This may save legal fees and stress.
   - You have more control over the outcome rather than leaving it all in the judge's hands.
2. **Disadvantages**
   - Some people might feel pressured or rushed.
   - Make sure you do not sign any deal unless you truly understand and accept it.
3. **Stay Alert**

- Listen carefully to any proposal. Ask questions if you are unsure.
- Do not let anyone bully you into a quick agreement. You can always say you need more time to think or speak to a legal advisor.

If you reach a fair agreement, the lawyers usually draft it in writing, and the judge might approve it without further court battles. If you cannot agree, you return to the courtroom.

13.12 Finalizing Court Orders

When the judge makes a decision, it is usually put into a written court order. This is a legally binding document:

1. **Read It Carefully**
   - Double-check that it matches what the judge stated. Sometimes errors happen in drafting.
   - If something seems incorrect, tell your lawyer or the court clerk immediately.
2. **Understand the Terms**
   - If it says you must pay a certain amount each month, know the due dates and method of payment.
   - If it sets a visitation schedule, note the specific times and pickup/drop-off locations.
3. **Keep a Copy Handy**
   - You may need to show it to a school, a landlord, or other institutions.
   - Store a copy in a safe place and consider keeping a digital version if that is allowed.
4. **Following Up**
   - If your spouse disobeys the order, you might have to file a motion to enforce it. This means going back to court to show that they are not following the judge's instructions.

Court orders bring clarity and finality to disputes, at least for the moment. However, life changes can still lead to adjustments down the road.

13.13 Extra Suggestions for a Smoother Court Experience

- **Arrive Early**: Being rushed can add panic. Aim to be at least 30 minutes early.
- **Keep Emotions in Check**: If you feel tears or anger building, breathe. Remember you want to appear calm and reasonable.
- **Observe Before Your Turn**: If you get a chance, watch a couple of other cases. You might see how the judge handles things and learn from others' mistakes or successes.
- **Stay Polite to Everyone**: From the bailiff to the court clerk, a respectful tone can go a long way.
- **Ask for Clarification**: If the judge says something you do not understand, politely say, "Your Honor, I am not clear on that. Could you please explain?" It is better to ask than to guess.

13.14 Mental Preparation for Court

1. **Visualize the Process**
   - Walk yourself mentally through checking in, speaking calmly, and leaving feeling that you did your best.
   - This reduces fear of the unknown.
2. **Plan for Support**
   - Ask a friend or family member to come with you for moral support. They might wait outside or in the gallery if allowed.
   - After the hearing, you could meet them for lunch or coffee to decompress.
3. **De-Stress Techniques**
   - Use calming strategies the night before: a warm bath, light reading, or relaxing music.
   - Avoid too much caffeine on the morning of court; jitters can make you more anxious.

Confidence grows when you feel prepared. Treat court like an important meeting: do your homework, know your goals, and present yourself well.

13.15 Common Myths About Court

- **Myth 1**: "The Mother Always Wins."
    - In many places, courts focus on the child's best interest, not on stereotypes. While mothers often get primary custody, fathers can also win custody if the evidence supports that arrangement.
- **Myth 2**: "Judges Are Always Harsh."
    - Judges aim to be fair. They can be stern if people behave poorly or disregard court orders, but they are not there to punish you needlessly.
- **Myth 3**: "You Will Get All You Ask For If You Prove Your Spouse's Fault."
    - Some areas have no-fault divorce rules, so personal blame may not sway the property or support outcome. It depends on local laws and the nature of the dispute.
- **Myth 4**: "If You Represent Yourself, You Will Lose."
    - While having a lawyer can help, many people successfully represent themselves by being organized, polite, and informed.

Understanding these myths helps you keep realistic expectations.

13.16 Feeling Empowered After Court

Whether the judge rules in your favor fully or partially, remind yourself that showing up and standing for your rights is an accomplishment. You have participated in a formal process, stated your case, and respected the law. This experience can be tough, but it also shows your ability to handle serious matters.

- **Track Court Dates and Outcomes**: Keep a record of what happened, who said what, and the final decision.
- **Plan Next Steps**: If the ruling is final, focus on adjusting to it. If you have follow-up tasks (like paying or receiving support), set reminders.
- **Give Yourself Space**: Court can be draining. Try to schedule time to rest or do something pleasant afterward.

Going through court can feel like a major hurdle, but it is also a step forward in concluding legal issues. Once it is behind you, you can put more energy into rebuilding your life, free from constant uncertainty about the legal side of things.

13.17 End-of-Chapter Summary

- **The Courtroom Layout**: Judge, court staff, lawyers, and you.
- **Preparation Steps**: Filing correct documents, organizing evidence, and planning arrival.
- **Courtroom Behavior**: Speak politely, do not interrupt, keep calm body language.
- **Cross-Examination**: Stay respectful, provide short answers, avoid guessing.
- **Possible Outcomes**: Immediate ruling, delayed decision, or extra requests from the judge.
- **If You Disagree with the Ruling**: Talk to a lawyer about appeals or future modifications.
- **Threats or Intimidation**: Protect yourself with documentation, official help, and by telling the court.
- **Self-Representation**: Learn the procedures, stay organized, and stay polite.
- **Myths vs. Reality**: Acknowledge common misunderstandings about how court works.
- **Empowerment**: Court can be stressful, but handling it well can boost your confidence for the next stages of your life.

By taking these court procedures step by step, you reduce panic and stand up for what matters. In the next chapter, we will look at "Staying Calm," focusing on deeper techniques to keep yourself steady during and after big conflicts like court cases.

CHAPTER 14

Staying Calm

Life during and after a divorce can feel like a whirlwind of emotions. Court hearings, money issues, parenting disputes, or social changes may pile up. In stressful moments, it is easy to feel overwhelmed. This chapter focuses on ways to maintain calm. It includes practical tips for stress reduction, mindful habits, and mental health support. You do not need special tools for most of these methods. They rely on simple techniques that can help you face each day with more steadiness and less panic.

14.1 Why Calmness Is Important

1. **Clear Thinking**
   - High stress can block logical thought and lead to mistakes. When you calm down, you can solve problems better and make wiser choices.
2. **Physical Health**
   - Stress can cause headaches, muscle tightness, and poor sleep, which can weaken the body over time. Staying calm can reduce these symptoms.
3. **Relationships**
   - Anger or panic can strain ties with children, friends, or family. A calm approach improves communication and helps keep trust.
4. **Emotional Reserve**
   - Life after divorce often brings unexpected issues. Having calm energy in reserve helps you adapt when new challenges appear.

Maintaining calm is not about ignoring problems; it is about having a clear mind to tackle them. It also lowers the constant tension that might hinder your daily life.

14.2 Recognizing Early Signs of Stress

To stay calm, first notice when stress begins:

1. **Body Clues**
    - Racing heartbeat, sweaty palms, or tight shoulders can be early signs you are getting anxious.
    - Stomach discomfort or shallow breathing might also appear.
2. **Mental Patterns**
    - Repetitive worrying or imagining worst-case scenarios can signal you are feeling tense.
    - Unusual irritability or struggling to focus can also be a clue.
3. **Behavior Changes**
    - Overeating, skipping meals, or reaching for substances (like alcohol) more often can indicate stress.
    - Withdrawing from friends or snapping at people can be a sign.

If you catch these signals early, you can pause and use a calm-down strategy before stress worsens. Awareness is the first step toward managing pressure.

14.3 Quick Calming Techniques

1. **Five-Count Breathing**
    - Breathe in for a count of five, hold for two, then breathe out for five. Repeat for a minute.
    - This slows the heartbeat and eases tight muscles.
2. **Progressive Muscle Relaxation (PMR)**
    - Sit or lie comfortably. Tense your feet muscles for a few seconds, then relax. Move upward to calves, thighs, hands, arms, and so on.
    - By the time you reach your head, many tension spots ease.
3. **Grounding Exercise**
    - Notice five things you can see, four things you can touch, three things you can hear, two things you can smell, and one thing you can taste.
    - This keeps you focused on the present instead of spiraling into "what-if" thoughts.
4. **Shake It Out**

- Gently shake your hands, roll your shoulders, or wiggle your legs to release built-up tension.
- This can look silly, but it can reduce that "on edge" feeling quickly.

These methods take only a few moments. Practicing them often builds a habit of calming yourself when trouble arises.

14.4 Longer Calming Rituals

For deeper relaxation, try activities that take more time:

1. **Daily Walk**
   - Even 15 minutes around the block can lower stress hormones. Notice the sky, trees, or local sights instead of focusing on problems.
2. **Warm Bath**
   - Dim the lights, use simple bath salts or gentle music. Soak for 10–20 minutes if possible.
   - Let your mind drift. If worries pop up, remind yourself this is your break.
3. **Gentle Stretch Routine**
   - Spend 10 minutes stretching your arms, back, hips, and legs. This can loosen muscles stressed by tension.
4. **Quiet Reading**
   - Pick a book that is calming or uplifting (not about divorce or conflict). Even short reading sessions can transport your mind somewhere else.
5. **Simple Hobby Time**
   - If you have a hobby, set aside 20–30 minutes to engage in it without distractions. This can slow your thoughts and provide a sense of achievement.

Rituals create a daily or weekly pause. They remind you that, despite chaos, you can find small moments of peace.

14.5 Mindset Shifts That Lower Stress

1. **Focus on Solutions, Not Blame**
    - It is easy to be angry at your spouse or even at yourself, but constant blame prolongs tension. Aim to find ways forward. Ask, "What can I do next?"
2. **Small Steps**
    - If the entire situation feels huge, break tasks into smaller steps. Tackle them one by one. For instance, if you have debt, start with calling one creditor or setting up one payment plan.
3. **Positive Self-Talk**
    - Change "I can't handle this" to "I can handle one part of this right now."
    - Remind yourself of past challenges you overcame. Those moments show you can face new problems too.
4. **Accept Imperfection**
    - Perfectionism piles on stress. Real life is messy, especially after a divorce. Doing your best is enough. If you slip, you can try again.

A calmer mind often grows from choosing how you think. While outside events can be unfair, focusing on practical next steps can keep you grounded.

14.6 Reducing Triggers in Your Environment

Sometimes, the environment can raise stress:

1. **Limit Negative Media**
    - Constant news about disasters or drama can heighten anxiety. Give yourself permission to switch off the TV or step away from social media.
2. **Declutter**
    - Messy spaces can add to mental overload. Tidy one corner or one drawer at a time. A simpler environment can feel more peaceful.
3. **Soothing Sights**
    - If possible, add small items that make you happy—like a plant, a calming image, or soft lighting.

- If you have painful reminders (like framed pictures from the marriage), store them away if they trigger sadness.
4. **Manage Noise**
    - Loud or continuous noise can raise stress. Consider using earplugs or playing gentle background sounds if you cannot control outside noise.

Changing your surroundings, even in small ways, can ease tension over time.

14.7 Communication Choices That Prevent Panic

How you talk to others can help you stay calm or worsen stress:

1. **Use "I" Statements**
    - Saying "I feel worried when…" or "I need some space right now" can reduce conflicts. It focuses on your feelings instead of blaming the other person.
2. **Ask for Time-Outs**
    - If a phone call with your spouse or a family member gets too heated, say, "I'm feeling upset. Let's pause this conversation and continue when we're calmer."
3. **Written Communication**
    - If speaking in person or on the phone creates arguments, consider sending emails or texts. Keep them brief and polite. This gives you time to craft your words carefully.
4. **Active Listening**
    - Even when you disagree, try to hear what the other person is saying. Often, conflict eases if people feel heard.

Better communication can prevent fights from becoming shouting matches. It can also make problem-solving easier.

14.8 Physical Health for Mental Calm

Keeping your body in good shape supports a calmer mind:

1. **Regular Meals**
   - Skipping meals can cause low blood sugar, leading to irritability. Plan simple, balanced meals or quick snacks like fruit, yogurt, or nuts.
2. **Hydration**
   - Dehydration can create headaches and fatigue, which add to stress. Keep water handy and sip throughout the day.
3. **Enough Sleep**
   - Sleep is essential for mood regulation. If you struggle with insomnia, try a consistent bedtime, reduce caffeine in the evening, and turn off screens an hour before bed.
4. **Gentle Exercise**
   - Exercise releases endorphins, which help you feel better. Even short sessions of home workouts or brisk walking can lift your mood.

When the body feels supported, the mind often manages stress more smoothly.

14.9 Limiting Interaction with Toxic People

Some individuals provoke stress no matter how hard you try to be calm. This might include certain relatives, acquaintances, or even old friends who thrive on drama:

1. **Set Boundaries**
   - Politely let them know you cannot engage in long, negative calls or chats. Keep contact minimal or focused on necessary topics.
2. **Change the Topic**
   - If they begin gossiping or complaining, steer the conversation to neutral ground. If that fails, end the interaction with a polite statement like, "I have to go now, thanks for understanding."
3. **Support Elsewhere**
   - Seek out calmer, kinder people. If you have few friends, look into support groups or online communities where folks share helpful tips and uplifting discussions.

You have the right to protect your peace. It is not rude to limit time with those who constantly bring tension.

14.10 Handling Panic Attacks or Extreme Anxiety

In some cases, stress can build to panic attacks:

1. **What They Feel Like**
   - Intense fear or sense of doom, pounding heart, shortness of breath, or dizziness.
   - You might worry you are dying or losing control, but panic attacks usually peak within minutes and then subside.
2. **Coping Steps**
   - Breathe slowly: in through your nose, out through your mouth.
   - Remind yourself, "This will pass. I'm not in real danger."
   - Sit down or lie down if possible, close your eyes, and focus on your breathing.
3. **Seek Help**
   - If panic attacks happen often, speak to a counselor or doctor. Therapy and sometimes medication can help manage severe anxiety.

Panic attacks are scary but not life-threatening. With practice, you can lessen their frequency and intensity.

14.11 Using Professional Support for Calm

Professional help can be a game-changer when stress feels overwhelming:

1. **Therapists or Counselors**
   - They can teach coping methods, help you work through deeper issues, and provide a judgment-free zone to express worries.
2. **Support Groups**
   - You may find divorce-specific or stress-management groups in your area. Hearing from others in similar situations can reduce feelings of isolation.
3. **Social Workers**
   - In some communities, social workers help with problem-solving, connecting you to resources like housing, healthcare, or child care assistance.

4. **Doctors**
   - If stress is harming your health, consult a physician. They might test for issues like thyroid problems or anemia, which can worsen anxiety or depression.

Seeking help is not weakness. It is an active step in caring for your well-being.

14.12 Mindful Living in Everyday Tasks

Mindfulness is about paying full attention to the present moment:

1. **Eating Slowly**
   - Notice the flavors, textures, and smells. Put down the fork between bites. This can calm racing thoughts.
2. **Showering with Awareness**
   - Feel the water on your skin, notice its temperature, and let each muscle relax.
3. **House Chores**
   - Instead of rushing, do them at a manageable pace. Be aware of each motion, whether you are folding laundry or washing dishes.
4. **Driving**
   - Focus on the road, the scenery, and your breathing. Turn off the radio if it distracts you. Keep your mind on the present act of driving.

By adding mindfulness to daily routines, you reduce mental "clutter" and bring moments of peace into ordinary tasks.

14.13 Teaching Children Calm Strategies (If You Have Kids)

Children can also feel tension from the changes after a divorce:

1. **Simple Breathing Exercises**
   - Show them how to breathe in like smelling a flower and breathe out like blowing out a candle.
2. **Quiet Corners**

- Create a small, cozy spot with cushions where they can sit when they feel upset. Let them color, read, or just rest.
3. **Routine and Predictability**
   - Children feel safer with regular mealtimes or bedtime. Consistency helps them stay calmer.
4. **Active Play**
   - Encourage outdoor activities, dancing, or even playing tag. Physical movement can release pent-up stress.

When kids learn calm strategies, it also lowers stress in the home. They see how you handle tension and often follow your lead.

14.14 Balancing Alone Time and Social Time

Too much alone time can lead to loneliness, but too many social demands can exhaust you:

1. **Know Your Preferences**
   - If you are an introverted person, you might need quiet hours to recharge. If you are extroverted, you might feel better with supportive friends around.
2. **Plan Visits Wisely**
   - Invite a friend over for tea or schedule a call. But avoid cramming too many social events into one day.
3. **Healthy Boundaries**
   - If you live with others, let them know you need a break sometimes. You can say, "I'll be in my room for a bit. I just need some quiet."
4. **Avoid Isolation**
   - While solitude can be soothing, cutting off people entirely can worsen depression. Keep a balance by checking in with at least one person you trust each week.

Finding your ideal balance can stabilize your moods and keep stress at bay.

14.15 Spiritual or Reflective Activities

If you have a faith or a sense of spirituality, you might gain calm from:

1. **Prayer or Meditation**
   - Spending a few minutes in prayer or quiet reflection can slow down racing thoughts.
   - If you are not religious, simple meditation apps or guided breathing can offer similar benefits.
2. **Reading Uplifting Texts**
   - This could be religious scripture or motivational books. Pick passages that bring comfort, not guilt or fear.
3. **Visits to Peaceful Places**
   - Churches, temples, or gardens can be calm spots. You do not have to attend services if that is not your style. Sitting quietly can soothe the mind.
4. **Small Acts of Kindness**
   - Doing something kind for someone else, like helping a neighbor or donating clothes, can shift focus from your stress to positive feelings.

Reflective practices can center you, giving a sense of purpose or calm when life feels hard.

14.16 Keeping a Stress Journal

A journal dedicated to stress management can track patterns and progress:

1. **Record Stress Events**
   - Note the date, what happened, and how stressed you felt on a scale of 1–10.
2. **Identify Triggers**
   - Over time, you may see that certain times of day, activities, or people trigger your stress.
3. **Note Coping Actions**
   - Write what you did to calm down. Did it help? If not, what else might you try next time?

4. **Acknowledge Improvements**
   - As weeks pass, you might see that your stress number drops faster or that certain triggers bother you less.

By studying your own patterns, you learn which methods are most effective for you and which situations need extra care.

14.17 Building a Personal Calm "Kit"

You can gather a small set of items or ideas that quickly bring relaxation:

1. **Physical Objects**
   - A stress ball, a smooth stone, or a small plush toy that you can hold when anxious.
   - Headphones for soothing music or nature sounds.
2. **Soothing Scents**
   - A mild lotion or essential oil with a pleasant fragrance (like lavender or chamomile) can lower tension when sniffed lightly.
3. **Written Reminders**
   - A note card with calming words or short affirmations. For example: "I am steady," "I will get through this," or "One step at a time."
4. **Tech Tools**
   - An app that plays calming music or guides you through meditation.
   - A folder on your phone with encouraging photos or saved messages from friends.

Keep this "kit" in your purse, car, or a corner of your home. When you feel anxiety rising, reach for it.

14.18 Incorporating Humor for Stress Relief

Laughter can be a powerful stress fighter:

1. **Watch Comedy**
   - Short clips or stand-up routines can shift your mood. Even a few minutes of genuine laughter can release tension.

2. **Share Funny Stories**
   - Talk to friends or family members who have a good sense of humor. You might trade silly events from your week.
3. **Avoid Mean Humor**
   - Sarcastic or hurtful jokes can worsen stress or create conflicts. Go for lighthearted material that uplifts.
4. **Laugh at Small Mishaps**
   - If you spill coffee or forget something minor, see if you can gently laugh at your own error instead of scolding yourself. This approach can keep small problems from becoming major stressors.

Humor does not cure all issues, but it can give you a refreshing mental break.

14.19 Planning for Tough Days

You may have days when stress is unavoidable, such as a court date or a big deadline at work:

1. **Prepare in Advance**
   - The night before, lay out clothes, gather papers, and ensure you get decent rest. Reducing last-minute chaos can help you feel calmer in the morning.
2. **Use Support**
   - Ask a friend to check in on you that day or to drive you if you are worried about anxiety.
   - Let your child know you might be busy or a bit tense, but that you will still be there for them.
3. **Time Buffer**
   - Arrive early wherever you need to be. Rushing can multiply stress.
4. **Cool-Down Plan**
   - After the tough event, schedule something calming: a short walk in nature, a phone call with a supportive friend, or a comforting meal.

Having a plan can make a challenging day feel more manageable.

14.20 Accepting Help from Others

Some people find it hard to accept help, feeling they must do everything alone. But leaning on others can lower stress:

1. **Small Favors**
   - A neighbor might pick up groceries for you if you are swamped. A family member might babysit your child for an hour so you can rest.
2. **Emotional Support**
   - Talking with a trusted friend about your worries can lighten mental load.
   - If you feel vulnerable, choose someone you know handles information with care.
3. **Professional Services**
   - Sometimes paying for cleaning or meal prep is worth it if it frees you to rest or focus on bigger tasks.

Saying "yes" to help can free up your emotional energy to cope with the real challenges of rebuilding life after divorce.

14.21 End-of-Chapter Summary

- **Value of Calm**: Clear thinking, better health, and stronger relationships result from reducing stress.
- **Early Warning Signs**: Watch your body and behavior for signals of rising anxiety.
- **Quick Techniques**: Short breathing exercises and grounding methods can bring fast relief.
- **Longer Rituals**: Walks, baths, and hobbies offer deeper relaxation.
- **Mindset Shifts**: Focus on solutions, use positive self-talk, and accept imperfection.
- **Environmental Changes**: Tidy spaces, limit noise, and remove negative reminders.
- **Better Communication**: Use polite boundaries, written options, or time-outs to reduce conflict.

- **Healthy Choices**: Balanced eating, good sleep, and light exercise help your mind stay level.
- **Professional Support**: Therapists, doctors, or support groups can guide you through stress.
- **Daily Mindfulness**: Being present in tasks like eating or showering can calm your racing mind.
- **Humor and a "Calm Kit"**: Laughter and handy tools can rescue you in anxious moments.
- **Planning for Hard Days**: Prepare and plan a cool-down to face tough events with less panic.
- **Accepting Help**: Let others lighten your load when you need it.

Staying calm does not mean ignoring life's problems. Rather, it means facing them with steadiness so that stress does not control you. As you practice these methods, you may see that your anxiety spikes happen less often and fade more quickly. This newly found calm can help you handle the aftermath of divorce and future hurdles with more confidence. In the following chapters, we will look at other key elements of rebuilding your life, including how to date safely, how to advance in your work or career, and more practical steps to move forward.

CHAPTER 15

Dating Safely

Many women wonder if they should date again after divorce. Some feel excited at the thought of meeting new people, while others feel nervous or stressed. Both feelings are normal. This chapter will talk about deciding if you are ready, practical steps to stay safe, and how to avoid common problems. Dating can be a positive experience if you approach it thoughtfully and take care of your emotional and physical well-being.

15.1 Checking If You Are Ready

1. **Listen to Your Feelings**
    - Some people jump back into dating right away to avoid loneliness. Others wait a long time because they still feel hurt.
    - Neither approach is wrong if it works for you. The key is to ask yourself: "Am I looking for a healthy connection, or am I still dealing with pain?"
2. **Allow Time for Healing**
    - If you still feel strong anger or sadness about your marriage, give yourself time. Dating might mix old wounds with new confusion.
    - Healing does not have a set deadline. It could be a few months or more than a year. Everyone is unique.
3. **Think About Your Goals**
    - Do you want a serious relationship, or just casual companionship? Being clear about what you want can prevent misunderstandings later.
    - If you have children, consider how a new partner might affect them. You do not need to introduce every date to your kids. It may be wise to wait until you see if the relationship is stable.

15.2 Being Honest About Your Situation

1. **Disclosing You Are Divorced**
   - Many dating profiles have a section about relationship status. If you are divorced, it is usually best to mention it upfront. That way, you avoid surprises or awkward talks later.
   - You do not have to share details of your divorce, but a brief statement like "I was married, now divorced" sets a clear expectation.
2. **Addressing Children**
   - If you have kids, some people will be comfortable with that, and others may not. That is okay. Being open about having kids helps you find someone who respects your role as a parent.
   - You do not need to give out all the details about your kids, such as where they go to school, right away. Keep them safe by waiting until trust is built.
3. **Deciding What to Share**
   - There is no rule that says you must share every painful event from your marriage. If asked, you can say, "I'd rather not get into all the details right now."
   - Over time, in a serious relationship, you might share more. But in the early stages of dating, protect your emotional boundaries by keeping some things private.

15.3 Online Dating vs. Traditional Meeting

1. Online Dating

- Pros: A wide pool of people, convenience, you can chat before meeting in person.
- Cons: Some profiles are not honest, and you might deal with rude messages or wasted time.
- Safety Tip: Use a nickname or only a first name when setting up a profile. Never share your home address or work address. Meet in public if you decide to see each other in person.

2. **Traditional Ways**

- Meeting through friends, social events, or shared hobbies.
- Pros: You may have common interests, and there is some social proof if friends introduce you.
- Cons: Smaller pool of options, could feel awkward if it does not work out and you have mutual friends.

You can try both or stick to what feels comfortable. If you do go online, be cautious with personal information. If you meet someone at a local event, still take basic safety steps.

15.4 First Meetings and Safety

1. **Choose Public Places**
   - Cafés, casual restaurants, or well-lit public venues are best for a first date. You can leave easily if you feel uneasy.
   - Avoid letting a stranger pick you up at home. Drive yourself or use a trusted ride service.
2. **Tell a Friend**
   - Let a friend or family member know where you will be, who you are meeting (give them a photo or name if you have it), and when you plan to come home.
   - Check in with them after the date, so they know you are safe.
3. **Watch Your Belongings**
   - Keep your purse, phone, and drink in sight. Sadly, there are cases of people slipping harmful substances into drinks. Even on a first date, guard your safety.
4. **Pay Attention to Red Flags**
   - If the person tries to push you to go somewhere isolated or seems too intense, trust your gut. You have the right to leave or end the date at any time.

15.5 Spotting Warning Signs

1. Moving Too Fast

- If your date is talking about living together, marriage, or big plans right away, be cautious. Quick intensity can be a sign of manipulation or lack of balance.

2. Disrespectful Behavior

- Pay attention to how they treat waitstaff, talk about ex-partners, or respond to disagreements. If they are rude, controlling, or dismissive, that is a warning sign.

3. Lack of Respect for Boundaries

- If you say "I am not comfortable doing that," and they ignore you or keep pushing, that is not a good sign.

4. Verbal or Physical Harm

- Any threat or actual harm is a deal-breaker. No excuses. If someone is yelling, insulting, or frightening you, leave.

15.6 Dating with Children in Mind

1. **When to Introduce a New Partner**
   - Many experts suggest waiting at least a few months of steady dating before letting your kids meet a new partner. This prevents confusion if the relationship ends quickly.
   - Children might get attached, and then feel hurt if the person disappears.
2. **Short First Meetings**
   - If you decide the relationship is serious enough to introduce them, keep the initial meeting short and casual. A park or a short meal might work.
   - Avoid overnight visits or long trips together until you are very confident in the person's character.

3. **Look for Red Flags in Relation to Your Kids**
    - Observe how this person interacts with your children. Are they patient or annoyed by normal child behavior?
    - A caring and respectful approach is a must. If your kids show clear signs of discomfort, listen to them and investigate why.

15.7 Handling Emotional Ups and Downs

1. Mixed Feelings

- It is normal to feel excitement one day and guilt or worry the next, especially if you were married a long time.
- Give yourself permission to feel these emotions. You are stepping into a new phase of life.

2. Comparing New Dates to Your Ex

- Some comparison is natural, but try not to overdo it. The new person is not your ex-spouse. Focus on what is happening now, not past hurts.
- If you find yourself thinking about your ex constantly when you are with someone new, you might need more healing time before dating seriously.

3. Setting a Comfortable Pace

- You can control how often you want to see someone or how fast you want the relationship to grow. If you need space, communicate that gently.
- A caring partner should understand and respect your pace.

15.8 Physical Intimacy and Safety

1. **Consent and Readiness**
    - Never rush into physical intimacy because you feel pressured or to "move on." Only do what feels right for you.
    - If the other person cannot respect your "no," that is a serious issue.
2. **Protection**
    - If you decide to be intimate, use methods to prevent unplanned pregnancy or disease. Regular checkups can also help you stay safe.

- Do not rely solely on the other person's word about health. Take your own precautions.
3. **Emotional Considerations**
    - Intimacy can open emotional bonds. If you are not ready for the feelings that might follow, it might be wise to wait.
    - Know yourself: do you handle casual intimacy well, or do you grow attached easily? Understanding your personal style can help avoid heartbreak.

15.9 Online Privacy and Scams

1. **Sharing Personal Info**
    - Never share bank details, addresses, or other sensitive data with someone you just met online.
    - Be mindful of what you post on social media that a potential scammer could use against you.
2. **Romance Scams**
    - Sadly, some people pretend to be interested in you just to get money or personal details.
    - If someone you have never met in person asks for money or starts with sad stories wanting cash, it is a huge warning sign.
3. **Video Chats**
    - Before meeting, you can do a short video call. It helps confirm they are who they claim to be and not using fake photos.
    - Even with video confirmation, stay alert. Some people might still hide other details.

15.10 Deciding Not to Date Yet

1. **It Is Okay to Wait**
    - Some women find they are happier taking time for themselves, focusing on career or children, and enjoying peace.
    - Friends or relatives may push you to "get back out there," but the choice is yours.
2. **Handling Pressure**

- If someone says, "You should be dating by now," you can respond, "I appreciate your concern, but I'm comfortable with my current life."
- Do not let external voices force you into something you do not want.
3. **Exploring Other Social Options**
    - You can still meet new people without dating. Join clubs, volunteer, or attend community events. This can give social connection without the pressure of romance.

15.11 Balancing Dating and Personal Life

1. **Childcare Plans**
    - If you have kids, you need a plan for who watches them when you go on dates. This might be a friend, grandparent, or babysitter.
    - Keep your children's routine stable. If you have an agreed co-parenting schedule, use the times your ex has the kids to plan dates if possible.
2. **Work and Other Activities**
    - Do not let dating take over your entire schedule. Maintain your hobbies, exercise, or time with friends.
    - A balanced life can prevent you from becoming too emotionally dependent on a new relationship.
3. **Avoiding Burnout**
    - Dating can be draining if you meet too many people at once. It is okay to set a limit or pace yourself with fewer first dates per month.
    - Quality over quantity might save you energy and keep the process enjoyable.

15.12 Handling Breakups or Rejections

1. **Short-Term Disappointments**
    - Not every date will lead to something serious. Some might ghost you, or you might not feel the spark. That is normal.

- Try to see each attempt as practice in learning what you want.
2. **If You End It**
    - Be respectful and honest if you decide to stop seeing someone. A short, clear message like, "I appreciated our time, but I do not feel we are a match," is better than ghosting.
    - This also shows emotional maturity.
3. **Moving On**
    - A breakup after divorce can reopen old wounds. Remind yourself that this is part of the dating world, not a final statement about your worth.
    - Lean on friends or family for support if you feel down.

15.13 Staying True to Yourself

1. **Values and Standards**
    - Know your deal-breakers and your must-haves. Do not compromise on major values like honesty or respect.
    - If someone mocks your boundaries, that is not a healthy match.
2. **Personal Growth**
    - Dating is not just about finding someone new; it can be about discovering more about who you are now.
    - Notice how you react in different situations. Learn from each experience.
3. **Confidence Booster**
    - Even if you do not find a long-term partner right away, meeting new people and trying new activities can boost your self-esteem.
    - You realize that you have much to offer, and you deserve kindness.

15.14 Surprising Pointers for Smart Dating

- **Check Public Records**: If you feel uneasy, you can do a quick online search of public records or social media. This is not about snooping, but basic safety.
- **Group Dates**: Early on, consider group activities instead of one-on-one, especially if you have any doubt.

- **Listen to Friends' Observations**: Sometimes close friends see warning signs you might miss. If they express worry, hear them out calmly.
- **Set Time Boundaries**: If you have only a little free time, keep the first date short, like an hour for coffee. If it is going well, you can schedule a longer second date.
- **Know Local Resources**: In case you face harassment or intimidation, be aware of hotlines or local support groups for women.

15.15 End-of-Chapter Summary

- **Check Readiness**: Ensure you are not dating just to avoid loneliness. Wait until you feel emotionally prepared.
- **Honesty**: Be open about your status as divorced and a parent if you have kids.
- **Safe Meetings**: Choose public places, tell a friend, and watch for red flags.
- **Emotional Caution**: Avoid rushing intimacy. Watch for signs of disrespect or controlling behavior.
- **Kids and Dating**: Introduce a new partner to your children slowly, only when you trust the situation.
- **Balance**: Keep your own life and boundaries, and do not let dating consume all your time.
- **Rejections**: They happen. View them as part of the process, not a reflection of your worth.
- **Confidence**: Healthy dating can remind you of your strengths. Be true to your values.

Dating after divorce can be a chance to meet people who respect and value you. It is not always easy, and there may be awkward or disappointing moments, but staying safe, honest, and patient can make the process more positive. In the next chapter, we will explore "Work and Career," looking at ways to strengthen your job skills, find new opportunities, and build a stable financial base for your future.

CHAPTER 16

Work and Career

After a divorce, many women face changes in their work life. You might need a better job to pay the bills, or you might want to return to a career you paused. This chapter covers how to refresh your skills, look for new opportunities, and balance work with personal responsibilities. It also addresses issues like feeling unsure about your abilities or worrying about taking a new path. Work and career can offer financial stability and a sense of purpose, both of which are valuable when rebuilding after divorce.

16.1 Assessing Your Current Situation

1. **Income vs. Expenses**
   - First, compare how much you earn each month with your bills. If you see a gap, you know you need more income. If you break even but feel stuck, you might explore ways to increase earnings or find a more fulfilling job.
2. **Work Experience**
   - List your past roles, skills, and achievements. Even if you have been out of the workforce, think about volunteer work or skills gained from managing a home, raising kids, or community involvement.
   - These can be used on a resume to show reliability, communication skills, or budgeting.
3. **Future Goals**
   - Ask yourself: Do I want to stay in my current job long-term, or do I see a different path? Am I aiming for a promotion, or do I want to switch fields entirely?

A clear picture of where you stand can guide your next steps, helping you set practical goals.

16.2 Updating Skills or Education

1. **Short Courses or Certificates**
   - Many community colleges or online platforms have short programs that teach specific skills (like bookkeeping, coding, or medical billing).
   - These courses can often be done in a few months, boosting your qualifications without a full degree.
2. **Higher Education**
   - If you want a degree, explore financial aid, scholarships, or part-time programs. Some schools have evening or weekend classes for working adults.
   - If you have children, ask about on-campus childcare or flexible scheduling.
3. **Digital Skills**
   - Basic computer skills (like Microsoft Office or Google tools) are needed in many jobs. You can watch free online tutorials to strengthen your abilities.
   - Social media or basic website knowledge can also open doors if you want a job in marketing or administration.
4. **Language Skills**
   - If you speak more than one language, highlight it on your resume. If not, consider learning a new language if it is valued in your region or industry.

Upgrading your skills can be done step by step. Even small improvements might lead to higher pay or better job options.

16.3 Job Hunting Methods

1. **Online Platforms**
   - Sites like LinkedIn, Indeed, or local job boards list many openings. You can filter by location, pay level, or role.
   - Be sure to tailor your resume to each application, using keywords from the job description.
2. **Networking**

- Talk to friends, family, or neighbors about your job hunt. Someone might know of a position that suits you.
- Attend local career fairs or community events where employers meet potential hires.

3. **Temp Agencies**
   - Temporary or contract work can be a quick way to earn money and gain new experience. Some temp jobs turn into permanent positions if you do well.
4. **Direct Approaches**
   - If you see a company you admire, check their website for job postings. Sometimes, sending a polite inquiry can work, especially for small businesses.

16.4 Crafting a Strong Resume and Cover Letter

1. **Resume Basics**
   - Keep it clear and concise (usually 1-2 pages).
   - Use bullet points to list tasks and achievements. Include measurable results if possible (like "Managed a budget of $5,000" or "Supervised a team of 3 people").
2. **Highlight Transferable Skills**
   - Even if your experience was not in a formal job, mention skills like organizing events, managing schedules, or handling finances.
   - Employers often care about good communication, teamwork, and dependability.
3. **Cover Letter Tips**
   - Address it to the correct person if possible.
   - In one page, explain why you want the job and how you can help the company. Keep it positive and show genuine interest.
4. **Proofreading**
   - Spelling or grammar errors can hurt your chances. Ask a friend or use online tools to check before sending your documents.

A well-prepared resume and cover letter can make you stand out, even if you have gaps in your work history.

16.5 Interviews: Preparation and Confidence

1. **Research the Company**
   - Before an interview, learn about the company's products, services, or mission. This shows genuine interest.
   - Think of a couple of questions you can ask them, such as "What qualities help someone succeed here?"
2. **Mock Interviews**
   - Practice common questions like "Tell me about yourself" or "What is your biggest strength?"
   - Rehearse with a friend or family member. Feedback can help you improve your answers and tone.
3. **Dress Appropriately**
   - You do not need expensive clothes, but choose neat, clean attire that fits the company's style. If unsure, lean toward formal rather than casual.
4. **Body Language**
   - Maintain eye contact, sit up straight, and avoid fidgeting. Smile naturally when you greet the interviewer.
   - Listen carefully to questions. If you do not understand, politely ask for clarification.
5. **Handling Nerves**
   - Deep breathing beforehand can calm shaky feelings.
   - Remind yourself that an interview is a conversation, not an interrogation. They want to see if you are a good match, and you are checking if the job fits you too.

16.6 Balancing Work with Parenting (If You Have Children)

1. **Childcare Solutions**
   - Look for trusted daycares, after-school programs, or family members who can help.
   - Some employers offer flexible schedules or childcare benefits, so ask during the hiring process if that is an option.
2. **Time Management**
   - Plan your morning and evening routines. If you pack lunches or set out clothes the night before, you can reduce morning chaos.

- Keep a family calendar with everyone's activities and deadlines.
3. **Discussing Needs with Your Boss**
    - If you have regular hours you must pick up children, explain this politely. Many workplaces are flexible if they see you are a responsible team member.
    - If the employer is not understanding, you might consider a different job. A supportive work environment can make a huge difference.
4. **Self-Care**
    - Balancing children, a new job, and possibly legal tasks can be exhausting. Protect some personal time, even if it is just 15 minutes each evening to relax.

16.7 Handling Workplace Challenges

1. **Adjusting to a New Role**
    - If you have been out of work for a while, there may be a learning curve. Ask questions when unsure. Show willingness to learn.
    - Understand that mistakes can happen. Focus on improvement rather than feeling shame.
2. **Dealing with Difficult Coworkers**
    - Keep communication polite and professional. If you face repeated conflict, ask a supervisor for advice or consult human resources.
    - Do not let toxic behavior push you out. You have a right to a respectful work environment.
3. **Asking for Raises or Promotions**
    - Track your accomplishments. If you have saved the company money or improved efficiency, document it.
    - Request a meeting with your boss, calmly present your achievements, and show why you deserve higher pay or a better title.
4. **Harassment or Discrimination**
    - If you believe you are treated unfairly due to your gender, marital status, or other factors, note dates and details of incidents.
    - Report serious problems to HR or a trusted manager. If they do not help, you can seek legal advice.

16.8 Considering Self-Employment or Gig Work

1. **Freelancing**
   - If you have skills like writing, graphic design, or bookkeeping, you might find freelance jobs online.
   - This can let you work from home on your schedule. But you must handle your own taxes and health insurance.
2. **Consulting**
   - If you have expertise in a certain field (like marketing or education), you can offer consulting services to clients.
   - Build a simple website or LinkedIn profile to explain your services.
3. **Online Selling**
   - Some women sell handmade items or used goods on platforms like Etsy or eBay.
   - This can be a side income if you enjoy crafts or decluttering.
4. **Gig Platforms**
   - Driving for ride-share services, delivering groceries, or doing home tasks can bring immediate earnings.
   - Just be sure to factor in expenses like car maintenance and gas.

Self-employment has flexibility, but also risks. Make a plan before diving in, including how you will find clients or manage finances.

16.9 Confidence in the Workplace

1. **Overcoming Imposter Feelings**
   - You might worry you are not as skilled as others or that your break from formal jobs means you are behind. Remind yourself that you can learn. Everyone started somewhere.
   - Seek out mentors or colleagues who can guide you.
2. **Positive Self-Talk**
   - Replace "I can't do this" with "I will figure it out step by step."
   - Celebrate small wins privately. If you handle a tough project, give yourself credit.
3. **Learning Culture**
   - The workplace is not static. People learn new processes all the time. Embrace training or ask coworkers for tips.

- When others see you are open to learning, they often respect your effort.
4. **Body Language at Work**
    - Stand or sit up straight during meetings. Make eye contact when speaking. This signals confidence, even if you feel nervous inside.

16.10 Managing Stress on the Job

1. **Breaks and Boundaries**
    - Take short breaks to stretch or breathe if your schedule allows. Staring at a screen non-stop can increase anxiety.
    - If coworkers often dump extra tasks on you, learn to say, "I'd love to help, but my plate is full now."
2. **Avoid Office Drama**
    - Gossip or negative talk can add to stress. Politely excuse yourself if conversations turn toxic.
    - Focus on your tasks rather than rumors about coworkers.
3. **Balanced Goals**
    - Set realistic goals for each day or week. Do not push yourself to do the work of three people. That path leads to burnout.
4. **Talk to Someone**
    - If stress is high, confide in a friend, counselor, or support group. Sometimes just sharing your feelings helps you cope better.

16.11 Financial Growth from Your Career

1. **Emergency Fund**
    - As you earn money, try to save a small amount regularly. Even $20 a week can build up.
    - This fund can cover car repairs or surprise medical bills.
2. **Retirement Accounts**
    - If your employer has a 401(k) or similar plan, contribute if you can. Over the long term, small contributions can become big savings.
    - If self-employed, research IRAs or other retirement options.
3. **Debt Reduction**

- If you have credit card or other high-interest debt, pay more than the minimum each month if possible.
- Once debts are lower, your monthly budget feels more flexible.
4. **Advancement**
    - A higher-paying role or a promotion can help you afford more and save more. Keep an eye out for chances to move up.

Earning money is not just about surviving—it also opens doors for security and a better future.

16.12 Standing Up for Yourself at Work

1. **Valuing Your Time**
    - Sometimes managers or coworkers might assume you can work late or handle extra tasks for no extra pay. Learn to say no politely but firmly if it goes beyond your limit.
2. **Knowing Your Rights**
    - Understand local labor laws. If your employer violates break rules, pay rules, or discriminates against you because you are divorced, you can seek help from labor agencies or legal advisors.
3. **Being Assertive, Not Aggressive**
    - Speak firmly without yelling or insulting. For example, "I cannot take on this project alone given my current workload, but I can help by doing X if someone else does Y."
4. **Document Concerns**
    - If you see ongoing issues, keep a simple record of dates, times, and details. This could help if you need to file a complaint.

16.13 Surprising Tips for Career Growth

- **Join Groups**: Professional associations often have monthly meetings, job boards, or training sessions. You can learn and meet contacts in your field.
- **Online Learning**: Websites offer free or low-cost courses in coding, design, marketing, and more. You can expand your resume at home.

- **Informational Interviews**: Ask someone in a role you admire if you can meet for coffee to hear about their path. Many people enjoy sharing advice.
- **Personal Projects**: If you want to go into writing, design, or tech, create sample projects to show employers. It is proof of your skills.

16.14 Balancing Ambition and Personal Life

1. **Set Limits**
    - If you push too hard at work, you might have no time or energy for kids or yourself. Decide how much overtime is okay and how much rest you need.
2. **Plan Family Activities**
    - Schedule fun or relaxing times with kids or friends so work does not take over. Even a short weekend outing can refresh your mind.
3. **Ask for Support**
    - If you have relatives or friends nearby, see if they can help with after-school pickup once a week so you can focus on a major project.
    - Do the same for them if they need help. Mutual support can ease everyone's load.
4. **Know Your Motivation**
    - Earning more or achieving a promotion is good, but remember why you want it. Maybe it is to give your children a secure life or to feel proud of your achievements. Keep that reason in mind when challenges arise.

16.15 Future Planning in Your Career

1. **Regular Check-Ins**
    - Every few months, ask yourself if you are happy in your job. Are you learning and growing? Do you feel fairly paid?
    - If not, consider if it is time for a new role or more training.
2. **Long-Term Vision**

- Some women dream of owning a small business. Others want to climb the corporate ladder. Write down these dreams and steps to get there.
3. **Mentorship**
    - A mentor is someone more experienced in your field who can guide you. Many professionals are willing to help if you show interest and respect for their time.
    - A good mentor gives honest feedback and shares insider knowledge.
4. **Staying Open to Change**
    - Technology or the market may shift, so be ready to adapt. If your industry shrinks, explore how your skills can transfer to another area.

16.16 Overcoming Self-Doubt

1. **Remember Past Successes**
    - List times you solved a problem or got praise for a job well done. This can remind you of your ability.
2. **Take Calculated Risks**
    - Maybe that means applying for a position that seems slightly above your level. If you never try, you will not move forward.
3. **Separate Emotions from Facts**
    - Feeling unsure does not mean you cannot do the work. Check the facts: do you meet most job requirements? Then you have a real shot.
4. **Positive Role Models**
    - Look for stories or people who overcame big obstacles, especially other single moms or women who rejoined the workforce. Their paths can inspire you.

16.17 Moving Past Workplace Setbacks

1. **Rejection Happens**
   - Not every company will hire you. It is normal to get a few rejections. Do not see them as a personal failure.
   - Instead, ask politely if they can give any feedback to help you improve.
2. **Learn from Mistakes**
   - If you realize you stumbled in an interview or your resume had errors, fix it for next time.
   - If a job did not work out because of a skill gap, focus on gaining that skill.
3. **Stay Hopeful**
   - Even after multiple setbacks, keep applying. The right opportunity can appear when you least expect it.
4. **Protect Your Mental Health**
   - Job searches can be draining. Set aside time each day for something fun or relaxing to keep your mood steady.

16.18 End-of-Chapter Summary

- **Assess Your Work Goals**: Know if you need more income, want a better fit, or seek personal growth.
- **Upgrade Skills**: Use short courses, online tutorials, or higher education to boost your resume.
- **Job Hunt Strategies**: Combine online searches, networking, and temp agencies. Tailor your resume and cover letter for each application.
- **Interviews**: Prepare, dress properly, be honest, and stay calm.
- **Work-Life Balance**: If you have kids, plan schedules and communicate needs at work. Protect personal time to avoid burnout.
- **Handling Challenges**: Learn to say no, document issues, and know your rights. Harassment is never acceptable.
- **Self-Employment**: Consider freelancing or gig work if you want flexibility, but plan well.
- **Stay Confident**: Remember your achievements, keep learning, and be open to new roles.

- **Advance Financially**: An emergency fund and retirement savings can grow as you progress in your career.
- **Future Growth**: Regularly review your goals. Seek mentors and adapt to changes in the market.

A stable and satisfying work life can give you financial security and personal pride after divorce. Whether you aim for a promotion, launch a business, or simply find a supportive workplace, your career steps can help build a solid foundation for you (and your children, if you have them). In the coming chapters, we will cover topics like making a new home, setting healthy boundaries, renewing connections, and finally moving ahead with strength. Each part of the process helps shape a life that reflects your resilience and future hopes.

CHAPTER 17

Making a New Home

After a divorce, your living space can change in many ways. You might move to a smaller place, stay in the family home, or even share a place with relatives for a while. Making a new home is not only about finding a roof over your head. It is also about creating an environment that feels safe and welcoming. This chapter will explore practical steps to choose or shape your living space and how to handle common challenges. A comfortable home can support emotional healing and bring a sense of stability to you (and your children, if you have them).

17.1 Choosing Where to Live

1. **Budget Considerations**
    - List out all your monthly expenses—rent or mortgage, utilities, groceries, insurance. Compare them with your income. You want to ensure you can cover everything without major stress.
    - If money is tight, you might pick a smaller apartment or a shared living arrangement. This can be temporary until you rebuild finances.
2. **Location Factors**
    - If you work outside the home, think about commute times and transportation costs.
    - If you have children, consider school districts. A good school near home can simplify daily life.
    - Check local crime rates, availability of groceries or medical facilities, and other practical needs.
3. **Support Network**
    - Living closer to family or close friends can help if you need babysitting or someone to talk to.
    - On the other hand, some people need distance from certain relatives to reduce drama or conflict. Decide which is more beneficial in your case.
4. **Future Plans**

- If you expect changes (like a new job or possible relocation), a short-term lease might be wiser than buying a house.
- If you are ready for stability, buying a small home or condo could be an option. But remember maintenance costs when considering ownership.

17.2 Staying in the Former Marital Home

If you keep the home you shared with your ex-spouse:

1. **Financial Implications**
   - Can you afford the mortgage or upkeep alone? Sometimes a large house can be a burden if you are on a single income now.
   - Review property taxes, repairs, and utility costs. If it is too expensive, selling might bring relief and a financial boost.
2. **Emotional Impact**
   - Some women feel safe and happy staying in the familiar home. Others feel weighed down by memories.
   - If the house triggers sadness or anger, consider making changes, such as repainting rooms or rearranging furniture. New décor can help you feel it is truly your space.
3. **Legal Details**
   - If your divorce agreement states you are responsible for mortgage payments, ensure the house title and loan documents are correctly adjusted.
   - Check if your ex-spouse's name is still on the mortgage. If so, look into refinancing or other legal steps to remove them if that is part of your settlement.

17.3 Starting Over in a New Place

1. **Renting vs. Buying**
   - Renting provides flexibility. You can leave if you find a better job or want a bigger (or smaller) place in the future.

- Buying can build equity over time, but it is a major financial commitment. Remember closing costs, property taxes, and repairs.
2. **Roommates or Shared Housing**
    - Sharing a place with another single mom or a friend can cut costs. It can also offer companionship if you trust each other.
    - Communicate clearly about bills, cleaning responsibilities, and rules to avoid conflict.
3. **Downsizing Benefits**
    - A smaller space can be cheaper and easier to clean. Moving to a simpler home can free up time and money for other goals.
    - You can also sell or donate extra furniture, reducing clutter and earning a bit of cash.
4. **Emotional Fresh Start**
    - Moving can symbolize a new chapter in your life. Arrange your furniture in ways that make you feel relaxed. Pick soothing or uplifting colors.
    - Add small personal touches that reflect your tastes—art, cushions, or photos of moments that bring a smile.

17.4 Making the Space Feel Like Yours

1. **Decluttering**
    - Go through old possessions. Keep the essentials and items that bring you happiness. Let go of things tied to painful memories.
    - Selling or donating excess stuff can create breathing room. Fewer items can also make small homes feel bigger.
2. **Rearranging**
    - If you cannot afford new furniture, rearrange what you have. Sometimes a simple shift of the sofa or bed can give a room a fresh feel.
    - Hang new curtains or change throw pillows for a budget-friendly update.
3. **Personal Décor**
    - Choose a few décor pieces that resonate with you. A favorite painting, a cozy blanket, or a nice lamp can help you relax.

- If you have kids, let them decorate their own corner or bedroom with their favorite colors or posters.
4. **Scent and Lighting**
    - Air fresheners or lightly scented candles can shift the atmosphere. Pick calming scents like lavender or something mild you enjoy.
    - Good lighting makes a space feel inviting. Use warm lamps, fairy lights, or natural light if possible. Harsh overhead lighting can feel stressful.

17.5 Handling Children's Feelings About a New Home

1. **Involve Them in Decisions**
    - If you have kids, they might feel unsettled by the move. Let them pick small aspects of their room décor or where to place their bed.
    - This sense of control helps them adjust and see the new home as theirs too.
2. **Keep Some Familiar Items**
    - If they have a favorite blanket, poster, or toy, ensure it is easily accessible in the new place. This can bring comfort during the transition.
    - Routine matters. If you can maintain certain schedules (mealtime, bedtime), it can help them feel safe.
3. **Address Fears**
    - Children might worry about losing friends or adjusting to a new neighborhood. Listen to their concerns without dismissing them.
    - Reassure them they can invite friends over or stay in touch. Talk positively about new opportunities, like parks or community events.
4. **Patience with Emotions**
    - Some kids act out or become clingy after a move. This can be their way of showing stress.
    - Be patient, show extra attention, and if needed, involve a counselor if they struggle long-term.

17.6 Dealing with Ex-Spouse and Property Issues

1. **Dividing Belongings**
   - If you have not divided all household items yet, follow your divorce decree. Document what items go to whom to avoid disputes later.
   - Avoid arguments over small stuff. If it is not valuable or sentimental, it might be easier to let it go.
2. **Visits or Exchanges**
   - If your ex-spouse comes to your home for child pickups or drop-offs, establish clear boundaries. For example, they might wait outside or in a common area if you live in an apartment.
   - Keeping a neutral, polite tone can lower stress. If conflict arises, consider a public exchange spot or a third party to mediate.
3. **Safety Precautions**
   - In some cases, an ex may have been controlling or harmful. If so, change the locks, update security systems, and let trusted neighbors know to keep an eye out if something seems off.
   - Make sure your children understand basic safety rules (not answering the door to strangers, calling you or a safe contact if they feel scared).

17.7 Budget-Friendly Home Improvements

1. **Paint**
   - A fresh coat of paint is an inexpensive way to liven a room. Choose light or warm tones to make the space feel open.
   - If you rent, get permission from the landlord first. Some landlords might allow it, especially if you stick to neutral colors.
2. **Used Furniture and Décor**
   - Thrift shops, yard sales, or online marketplaces can have great deals. A little sanding or a coat of paint can transform old items.
   - Look for freebies in local "swap" groups if your community has them.
3. **DIY Projects**
   - Simple tasks like hanging shelves or repurposing wooden pallets can add character. Many short videos online show how to do small home fixes.

- Always be cautious with tools. If you are not sure you can handle it safely, ask someone experienced for help.
4. **Indoor Plants**
    - Plants can brighten a room, clean the air, and improve mood. Pick low-maintenance ones like snake plants or pothos if you are new to plant care.
    - If you have pets or kids, check which plants are non-toxic to keep everyone safe.

17.8 Emotional Meaning of Your Living Space

1. **A Place to Heal**
    - A calm home can act like a personal retreat when life outside feels overwhelming.
    - Small calming corners (a reading nook, a comfy chair with a blanket) can help you unwind.
2. **Self-Expression**
    - Your home is an extension of your personality. If you love art or bright colors, let that show. This is a chance to express yourself without worrying about a partner's opinion.
3. **Boundaries Within Your Home**
    - If you have children or roommates, you might need a private spot—a bedroom or small corner—where you can reflect, read, or just breathe quietly.
    - Even if you share a small space, a folding screen or a simple curtain can create a private area.
4. **Feeling Safe**
    - After a divorce, you want your home to feel secure. Check door locks, window latches, smoke alarms, and lighting around the entrance.
    - Feeling physically safe is vital to emotional well-being.

17.9 Hosting Friends or Family

1. **Social Connections**
   - Inviting friends or family over can help your new place feel more like home. It can also combat loneliness.
   - If you have limited space, a casual gathering is still possible. Make it simple with snacks or a potluck style.
2. **Setting Rules**
   - If certain relatives cause drama, you can keep visits short or meet them outside your home. Protect your peace.
   - Let guests know your boundaries, especially if you do not want them to bring up your ex or ask personal questions in front of your children.
3. **Kid-Friendly Gatherings**
   - If you have children, you might invite friends with kids. Keep the atmosphere light—maybe a simple board game or a craft activity.
   - This also helps your children see that life can still be fun and social after divorce.
4. **Celebrations**
   - You might mark smaller achievements at home, like finishing a course or starting a new job. Have a small treat or a quiet dinner with close friends.
   - This can reinforce that your home is a positive space where good things happen.

17.10 Dealing with Loneliness in a New Home

1. **Acknowledge the Change**
   - After divorce, it might feel strange not having someone else in the house, especially if your children are with your ex part of the time.
   - Recognize that loneliness is normal. It does not mean you made a mistake by splitting up.
2. **Fill the Silence**
   - Play music or podcasts you enjoy. Hearing voices or soothing sounds can make the space feel less empty.
   - Invite a friend over for a simple meal or a movie night occasionally.
3. **Stay Active**

- If the quiet at home feels too heavy, spend time at local events, libraries, or volunteer groups. Then come home to rest.
- Having plans outside can make you appreciate your calm space when you return.

4. **Pets**
   - If you love animals and can handle the responsibility, adopting a pet can bring companionship.
   - Ensure you have the time, budget, and permission from a landlord if you rent.

17.11 Organizing Important Documents

1. **Home Files**
   - Keep a folder for lease or mortgage papers, property tax bills, and insurance documents. Knowing where these are reduces panic if something goes wrong.
   - If you have any agreement with your ex about property or shared responsibilities, store those papers in this folder too.
2. **Digital Backups**
   - Scan vital records (like birth certificates, divorce decree) and save them to a secure cloud service or a flash drive.
   - This helps if you ever lose the physical copies in a move or emergency.
3. **Warranties and Manuals**
   - If you buy or inherit appliances, keep their manuals and warranties in one place. This makes repairs easier.
   - Label the cords or accessories to avoid confusion.
4. **Emergency Plan**
   - Have a simple plan for emergencies: where to go if there is a fire, who to call for plumbing or electricity issues, and so on.
   - Teach your children about basic safety procedures (dialing emergency numbers, leaving the house quickly if a smoke alarm goes off).

17.12 Creating a Calm Atmosphere

1. **Noise Control**
   - If neighbors are noisy, consider rugs or curtains that can absorb some sound. White-noise machines or soft music at night might help you sleep better.
   - Earplugs can be useful if you are in a crowded building.
2. **Managing Clutter**
   - It is easy for papers, toys, or clothes to pile up. Spend a few minutes each day putting things back where they belong.
   - A tidy space often feels calmer than a messy one.
3. **Nature Elements**
   - Even a small vase of flowers or a picture of a peaceful landscape can reduce stress.
   - If you have a porch or tiny outdoor area, a chair or bench can let you enjoy fresh air.
4. **Personal Rituals**
   - You might enjoy a quick meditation in the morning or lighting a small candle at dinner.
   - Rituals help mark your home as a place of self-care and well-being.

17.13 Handling Utilities and Maintenance

1. **Utility Services**
   - If you are moving, set up electricity, water, and internet ahead of time so you are not without them.
   - Compare providers if you have options. Sometimes you can find cheaper rates with a different company.
2. **Maintenance Schedules**
   - If you rent, ask your landlord how to report issues. Keep their contact details in an easy-to-find spot.
   - If you own your home, note when you should change air filters, clean gutters, or check the water heater. Regular upkeep can prevent bigger problems.
3. **Budget for Repairs**

- Even small repairs can cost money. Setting aside a little each month for home fixes can save stress when something breaks unexpectedly.
4. **DIY vs. Professional Help**
    - Some repairs, like unclogging a drain, are simple. Others, like electrical work, might need a professional for safety.
    - When in doubt, ask for help from someone with experience.

17.14 Surprising Ways to Make a Home Feel Better

- **Leave Shoes at the Door**: This keeps floors cleaner and helps you feel you are entering a relaxing space.
- **Try Soft Background Music**: Gentle tunes can lighten the mood, especially during chores.
- **Seasonal Touches**: A small seasonal decoration or a scented candle that matches the time of year can lift spirits.
- **Create a Vision Board**: Hang a bulletin board with images or quotes that inspire you—related to goals, travel, or just positive words.

17.15 End-of-Chapter Summary

- **Choosing Where to Live**: Think about budget, location, and future plans. Sometimes renting is better for flexibility, while buying can offer stability.
- **Staying or Moving**: If you keep the old home, be mindful of upkeep and emotional ties. A new place can be a fresh start.
- **Making It Yours**: Use simple décor, rearranging, or paint to create a comfortable environment. Declutter to reduce stress.
- **Children and Transitions**: Involve kids in small decisions. Keep routines to help them adjust.
- **Security and Boundaries**: Change locks if necessary, set rules for ex-spouse visits, and keep important documents organized.
- **Budget-Friendly Updates**: Paint, secondhand finds, and indoor plants can brighten a place without high costs.
- **Handling Loneliness**: Invite friends sometimes, keep the environment comforting, and consider a pet if it fits your life.

- **Maintenance**: Plan for utility bills, repairs, and daily tidying.
- **Personal Rituals**: Simple habits can create a sense of peace in your home.

Making a new home after divorce gives you a chance to shape a living space that reflects your values and needs. Whether small or large, rented or owned, your home can become a place of solace where you feel supported and at ease. In the next chapter, we will explore "Setting Healthy Boundaries," which helps protect your emotional space not just at home, but in all areas of life.

CHAPTER 18

Setting Healthy Boundaries

When going through a divorce, you may discover that people around you—family members, friends, even coworkers—want details or try to control your decisions. Setting healthy boundaries is a way to protect your emotional well-being and your time. Boundaries define what you find acceptable and how you expect others to treat you. This chapter explains how to establish those boundaries, communicate them politely, and handle reactions from people who might challenge them. Having clear boundaries can reduce stress and build stronger, healthier relationships moving forward.

18.1 Understanding What Boundaries Are

1. **Definition**
   - A boundary is a limit you set on how others can interact with you. It might involve what topics you do not want to discuss, how much time you can give, or behaviors you will not tolerate.
2. **Why They Matter**
   - Boundaries help you maintain control of your life. Without them, people may overstep, leaving you overwhelmed or resentful.
   - They also teach others how to respect your space, emotions, and responsibilities.
3. **Common Misunderstandings**
   - Some people see boundaries as "selfish" or "unkind." In truth, healthy boundaries are respectful. They prevent confusion and conflict because everyone knows the limits.
4. **Types of Boundaries**
   - **Physical**: Your personal space and comfort with touch.
   - **Emotional**: Topics or emotions you share, and how you react to others' emotions.
   - **Time**: How much time you can give to tasks, calls, or social events.
   - **Mental**: Your beliefs and freedom to have your own opinions without coercion.

18.2 Signs You Need Boundaries

1. **Feeling Drained**
   - If you constantly feel tired, stressed, or irritated after interactions with certain people, it could mean they are crossing your limits.
2. **Frequent Guilt or Obligation**
   - Do you say "yes" to favors because you feel guilty, even when you do not have the energy or resources? That is another sign.
3. **Anxiety About Encounters**
   - If you dread calls or visits from someone because they always dig into your personal life or demand too much, boundaries might help.
4. **Loss of Personal Identity**
   - When you never have time for your own needs or choices, and everyone else's demands come first, it indicates that your boundaries are weak or nonexistent.

Recognizing these signs can push you to establish or strengthen boundaries to protect your well-being.

18.3 Identifying Your Limits

1. **Self-Reflection**
   - Ask yourself: "What behaviors make me uncomfortable? In which situations do I feel used or upset?"
   - Think about times when you felt resentment or anger. Often, those feelings come from ignored limits.
2. **Values Check**
   - Know what is important to you—like honesty, respect, or personal space. If people violate these values, that is a boundary area.
3. **Time Boundaries**
   - How much time can you truly spare for phone calls, events, or helping others without damaging your own responsibilities?
   - If you are a parent or working multiple jobs, you might have limited free hours. Protect some of it for rest or things you enjoy.
4. **Emotional Boundaries**

- Decide how much detail you want to share about your divorce. You do not have to let everyone know the intimate reasons.
- If certain questions bother you, plan how to respond or politely redirect the topic.

18.4 Communicating Boundaries Politely

1. **Use Clear Language**
   - For instance, say, "I understand you want to know about my divorce, but I prefer to keep those details private," instead of giving vague hints.
   - "I need time for myself tonight" can be more effective than making excuses about being busy.
2. **Stay Firm but Kind**
   - You can be polite while still being direct. "I appreciate your concern, but I'm not comfortable discussing that," is clear.
   - If the person persists, repeat your statement calmly. Consistency shows you are serious.
3. **Offer Alternatives**
   - If a family member wants a long visit every weekend and you cannot handle that, suggest a shorter visit or a phone call midweek. That way, you are not shutting them out completely.
4. **Avoid Over-Explaining**
   - You do not owe lengthy justifications. A simple "No, I'm not able to do that" or "I need to think about it first" is often enough.
   - Over-explaining can invite arguments or guilt trips. Stick to the core message.

18.5 Boundaries with an Ex-Spouse

1. **Parenting Schedules**
   - If you share children, you will need some contact. Keep communication focused on the children's needs.
   - Decide the best method—maybe email or a parenting app. This reduces emotional tension compared to phone calls.

2. **Dropping By Unannounced**
    - Let your ex know you want scheduled pickups or drop-offs. State clearly that you do not appreciate surprise visits.
    - If they ignore this, do not let them in. Ask them to come back at the agreed time or meet in a neutral location.
3. **Avoiding Old Arguments**
    - If your ex tries to relive past conflicts, say something like, "I understand you're upset, but I'm not discussing that again. Let's stick to the current issue about the kids' schedule."
    - Shut down attempts to draw you into blame or personal attacks.
4. **Legal Restraints**
    - In severe cases, a restraining order might be necessary if the ex-spouse is harassing you or violating your space. Safety is top priority.
    - Consult legal authorities if you feel threatened.

18.6 Boundaries with Family

1. **Parents or Siblings**
    - Family members may pry into your divorce or tell you what to do.
    - You might say, "I know you care, but I need to make decisions in my own time. Thanks for understanding."
2. **Extended Relatives**
    - Some aunts, uncles, or cousins may gossip or judge. If a relative keeps pushing, you can limit contact or keep conversations surface-level.
    - Decide ahead how you will respond to personal questions—maybe a neutral phrase like, "I'm handling things fine, thank you," and change the subject.
3. **Handling Guilt Trips**
    - If a parent says, "You never visit anymore, you must not care," respond calmly: "I do care, but I have limited free time. Let's find a date that works for both of us."
    - Show empathy but do not let them manipulate you into ignoring your own limits.
4. **Family Events**

- If large gatherings cause stress (too many questions or unwanted drama), you can attend for a short while or skip occasionally.
- You can politely say, "I won't be able to stay long, but I wanted to stop by," and leave when you feel it's time.

18.7 Boundaries with Friends

1. **Different Opinions on Your Divorce**
    - Friends might try to give unsolicited advice or judge your choices. A simple "I appreciate your thoughts, but I have it under control" can help.
    - If they persist or criticize you harshly, you might need to see them less often.
2. **Time and Emotional Energy**
    - Some friends may rely on you for venting or constant help. While friendship is mutual support, watch out if it is only one-sided.
    - If you are drained, say, "I want to be there for you, but I'm at my limit today. Let's talk another time when I can give you my full attention."
3. **Social Activities**
    - After divorce, you might not enjoy certain events or bars you once went to as a couple. It is okay to say "no" to invites that do not fit your current comfort level.
    - Real friends will respect you if you explain you need quieter or different types of outings.
4. **Ending Toxic Friendships**
    - If a friend consistently lies, belittles you, or makes drama, it might be time to step away.
    - You can distance yourself slowly or, if needed, be direct: "I feel our friendship is unhealthy. I need some space now."

18.8 Boundaries at Work

1. **Personal Life at the Office**
   - Coworkers might ask about your divorce or personal matters. Decide what you want to share. "I prefer to keep personal issues private at work," is acceptable.
   - If you need certain flexibility (like picking up children), explain that professionally to your boss rather than sharing emotional details.
2. **Handling Overwork**
   - If colleagues keep piling tasks on you, politely say, "I'd like to help, but I have these other deadlines. Which task should be priority?"
   - Setting boundaries here prevents burnout and ensures you are not taken for granted.
3. **Avoiding Office Gossip**
   - Do not participate in rumor-spreading. If someone tries to dig into your divorce, calmly redirect the conversation to work topics.
   - Keep relationships at work positive and professional.
4. **After-Hours Contact**
   - If your boss or coworkers frequently message you in the evenings or weekends, decide how you will handle it. If it is not urgent, you can reply during work hours.
   - You might politely say, "I handle non-urgent emails when I'm back in the office."

18.9 Saying "No" without Guilt

1. **Direct Refusal**
   - "No, I can't do that" is enough. Adding "I'm sorry but…" can soften it, but do not add excuses that invite more pressure.
   - People who respect you will accept your answer. Those who push might be testing your boundary.
2. **Partial Agreement**
   - If you cannot do all of a favor, see if you can do a smaller part. For example, "I can't watch your dog all weekend, but I can do Friday night only."
   - This shows goodwill but still protects your main limit.
3. **Prioritize**

- You have limited time and emotional energy. Focus on tasks that are truly important or meaningful. Let go of extra requests that drain you.
4. **Self-Respect**
    - Remind yourself that saying "no" is not being unkind. It is safeguarding your resources to stay healthy and steady in your responsibilities.

18.10 Reactions from Others

1. **Anger or Shock**
    - Some people might get upset when you first set new boundaries, especially if they benefited from your lack of limits.
    - Stay calm. Repeat your boundary. Do not escalate into a fight. Their reaction is their problem, not yours.
2. **Guilt Trips**
    - They might say, "You've changed since your divorce. You're so distant now." You can respond with something like, "Yes, I am focusing on what I need right now. I still value you, but I need this space."
    - Acknowledge their feelings but stand firm.
3. **Testing Your Limits**
    - Some will test you to see if you really mean it. Continue to uphold your boundary. Consistency is key.
    - If they see you give in once, they might keep pushing.
4. **Positive Acceptance**
    - Good friends or family will eventually respect your boundaries, possibly even admiring your honesty.
    - New, healthier patterns of interaction can emerge, improving the relationship.

18.11 Boundaries with Your Children

1. **Respecting Personal Space**
   - If your child is old enough, explain that you also need some quiet time for reading or relaxation. This teaches them that parents are individuals with needs.
   - Show them how to knock before entering your room, especially if they are older.
2. **Time for Yourself**
   - Single parents can feel guilty taking time away from kids. But a short break can recharge you, so you can be more patient later.
   - Let your child know who will care for them (babysitter, grandparent) if you step out. They might initially resist, but they usually adapt.
3. **Age-Appropriate Conversations**
   - You do not need to share all divorce details with children. Keep adult topics off-limits. If they ask too many personal questions, say, "That's something for grown-ups to handle."
   - This boundary protects them from adult stresses they are not ready for.
4. **Consistent Routines**
   - Boundaries also include consistent bedtimes or rules about chores. Sticking to them gives children a sense of security.
   - If they push back, calmly remind them why these rules are in place.

18.12 Self-Boundaries and Self-Respect

1. **Limiting Negative Self-Talk**
   - Set a mental boundary against constant self-criticism. When you catch yourself thinking "I'm a failure," replace it with a kinder statement: "I made a mistake, but I can learn."
2. **Healthy Habits**
   - Decide on personal rules, like not working past a certain hour, or sticking to a reasonable bedtime. This boundary protects you from burnout.

- Keep track of how much you scroll social media if it makes you feel worse. A self-boundary could be "Only 15 minutes a day."
3. **Emotional Regulation**
    - If you feel your anger rising, take a step back before responding. This personal boundary prevents you from lashing out and later regretting it.
    - Calmly say, "I need a minute to think," and come back to the conversation when you are ready.
4. **Avoiding Overcommitment**
    - You may want to please everyone, but promising too much leads to stress. Learn to keep your schedule balanced.
    - If you want to help, be realistic about your capacity.

18.13 Handling Boundaries Online

1. **Social Media Privacy**
    - Avoid posting every detail of your divorce or personal life. Some things are best kept offline.
    - Adjust privacy settings so strangers or distant acquaintances do not see sensitive information.
2. **Online Communication**
    - If someone messages you non-stop, you can let them know you need time to respond.
    - If they harass you, block them. That is a digital boundary.
3. **Avoiding Triggering Content**
    - Unfollow or mute accounts that make you feel anxious, angry, or upset.
    - If social media is draining, set times of the day when you do not check it at all.
4. **Respecting Others' Boundaries**
    - If someone does not want their photo shared, respect that. Boundary respect goes both ways.

18.14 Reinforcing Boundaries Over Time

1. **Consistency**
   - People might forget or hope you changed your mind. Gently remind them, "I already mentioned I'm not discussing that," if they bring it up again.
2. **Adjust Boundaries**
   - As life changes, you might ease up on some boundaries or tighten others. For example, you might decide you can handle a bit more social time as you heal, or less if you get busier.
3. **Praise Yourself**
   - Give yourself credit when you hold firm. Boundaries take courage.
   - Notice if you feel lighter after standing your ground. That is a sign you made the right choice for your mental health.
4. **Learn from Mistakes**
   - If you break your own boundary (like over-sharing or letting someone walk over you), do not beat yourself up. Reflect on what happened and plan how to handle it better next time.

18.15 Unexpected Benefits of Boundaries

- **More Respect**: People often respect those who set clear limits, even if they react poorly at first.
- **Less Resentment**: You avoid hidden anger because you are no longer doing things out of guilt or pressure.
- **Better Self-Worth**: Knowing you can protect your emotional and physical space boosts confidence.
- **Healthier Relationships**: Interactions become more balanced and genuine because you are honest about your comfort levels.

18.16 End-of-Chapter Summary

- **What Are Boundaries?**: Guidelines that protect your time, emotions, and personal space. They prevent others from overstepping.

- **Signs You Need Them**: Feeling drained, resentful, or anxious about certain interactions.
- **Identifying Your Limits**: Reflect on what topics, behaviors, or demands bother you.
- **Communicating Clearly**: Use polite but firm language. No need to over-explain or apologize too much.
- **With Ex-Spouses**: Keep communication child-focused if you share parenting duties. Set rules for visits.
- **With Family and Friends**: Know how to handle prying, guilt trips, or unhelpful advice.
- **At Work**: Keep personal issues limited, and say no to extra tasks when your plate is full.
- **Saying "No"**: A direct, honest refusal can save you from burnout.
- **Handling Reactions**: Stay calm if people are upset. Consistency is key.
- **Online Boundaries**: Be mindful of what you share. Use privacy settings and block features as needed.
- **Self-Boundaries**: Protect your own health by limiting negative self-talk and overcommitting.
- **Long-Term Reinforcement**: Boundaries may need reminders, updates, and self-praise.

Healthy boundaries are essential for managing your new life after divorce. They let you control how others treat you and ensure you do not become overwhelmed. In future chapters, we will look at reconnecting with people in healthier ways, renewing friendships, and finally moving forward with greater strength. Each of these elements, combined with boundaries, will keep you on track to a more stable and satisfying post-divorce life.

CHAPTER 19

Renewing Connections

After a divorce, many women find their social circles change. Some friends may pull away or choose sides, and you may feel awkward around old social groups that still remind you of married life. It is common to sense a gap in your network of close contacts. This chapter explores how to renew existing friendships, build new ones, and strengthen ties with supportive people. It also looks at reconnecting in ways that fit your current needs and help you feel less alone. Healthy connections can give you a sense of belonging and comfort as you continue to rebuild your life.

19.1 Why Connections Matter

1. **Emotional Support**
   - When big life changes happen, having people around who listen and care can reduce feelings of isolation.
   - A kind friend or trusted family member can help you feel understood, especially on days when worries seem heavy.
2. **Practical Help**
   - Friends or relatives can offer guidance or tips—like recommending a good daycare, a local job lead, or a helpful mechanic.
   - They can also lend a hand if you need a babysitter, a ride, or someone to watch your pet in an emergency.
3. **Shared Joys**
   - Connections are not just about problem-solving. They are also about having people to laugh with, to share good news, or to enjoy a simple meal together.
4. **Personal Growth**
   - Talking with others can introduce you to new ideas or perspectives. A supportive conversation might open your mind to options you never considered before.

Having the right mix of people in your life can increase your sense of community and reduce loneliness. Even if your circle is small, quality relationships can matter more than quantity.

19.2 Reevaluating Old Friendships

1. **Friends You Grew Apart From**
   - Sometimes, close bonds formed during marriage can fade if those friends mostly related to you as a couple.
   - If you wish to stay in touch, try inviting them for coffee or a relaxed chat. See if the bond still feels comfortable without the couple-based dynamic.
2. **Ones Who Took Sides**
   - Some individuals pick your ex's side or judge you. That can hurt deeply. You might choose to let them go if they cannot respect your decision to divorce.
   - If they are open to listening to your perspective, you can try a calm conversation to clear the air. But do not push if they remain biased or harsh.
3. **Friends Who Supported You**
   - Notice who was there for you—who texted to check on you, who offered a shoulder when you felt down.
   - Show gratitude for their care. A simple "Thank you for being there" can deepen the bond.
4. **Ties That Need Space**
   - You might realize some people drain your energy or constantly bring negative vibes. If you find yourself anxious before seeing them, consider reducing contact or setting clearer boundaries.
   - Let them know you have limited emotional capacity right now. Real friends often understand.

19.3 Family Reconnections

1. **Repairing Strained Relationships**
   - Divorce can surface old family tensions or create new ones. If you want to reconnect with a relative, try sending a calm message or scheduling a short visit.
   - Share a bit about your life now, and politely maintain boundaries if they dig too far. Keep interactions respectful.
2. **Meeting Relatives with Caution**
   - Some family members might still be angry or disappointed about the divorce. Decide if you are ready to hear their opinions.

- If you prefer not to discuss the divorce, say so clearly. You can suggest topics like everyday life or common interests to steer the conversation elsewhere.
3. **Younger or Older Generations**
    - Sometimes older relatives can give perspective: they might have seen many challenges in their lifetime. Or younger siblings might lighten your mood with a fresh viewpoint.
    - Accept helpful guidance, but do not let them rule your decisions.
4. **Extended Family Events**
    - Weddings or holidays can feel awkward if your ex's family attends, or if you are not sure how people will treat you.
    - Plan ahead: decide how long you will stay, who you will talk to, and what you will do if conversation becomes tense. A short, polite appearance can work if you are not ready for a long gathering.

19.4 Building New Friendships

1. **Community Activities**
    - Joining local classes, workshops, or social groups can introduce you to people with shared interests.
    - Check community centers, libraries, or online community boards for cooking classes, book clubs, or exercise groups.
2. **Volunteering**
    - Helping at an animal shelter, food bank, or charity event can let you meet compassionate individuals who care about the same causes.
    - Volunteering can also boost your sense of purpose, shifting focus away from personal stress.
3. **Online Groups**
    - Some social media networks host local interest groups—like hiking clubs or game nights. Choose groups that match your hobbies or curiosity.
    - Always meet in public places if you decide to attend an in-person event with a group you found online.
4. **Parent-Focused Circles** (If You Have Kids)
    - School events, sports teams, or parent-teacher associations can help you meet other parents.

- Even a casual chat while waiting to pick up kids can evolve into a friendly connection over time.

19.5 Refreshing Your Social Skills

1. **Listening More**
   - Real friendship grows when people feel heard. Practice active listening: look at the speaker, nod or respond briefly, and avoid interrupting.
   - Summarize what they said to show you understand, like "It sounds like you've had a rough day."
2. **Asking Friendly Questions**
   - If you are shy or unsure how to keep a conversation, ask open-ended questions: "What do you enjoy about that hobby?" or "How did you get into this job?"
   - People love to share their stories. Genuine curiosity can build a bridge.
3. **Sharing Appropriately**
   - Balance is key. Ask about them, but also reveal some of your own thoughts or experiences—without going too deep into divorce details if you are not comfortable.
   - Find a middle ground: not too little, not too much.
4. **Handling Introversion vs. Extroversion**
   - If you are more introverted, aim for smaller get-togethers or one-on-one coffee meets. If you are extroverted, group activities might energize you.
   - Respect your comfort zone. Trying to be someone you are not can strain you.

19.6 Overcoming Fears of Judgment

1. **Feeling Self-Conscious About Being Divorced**
   - You might worry people judge you or pity you. In reality, many respect someone who made a hard decision for their well-being.
   - Focus on showing your genuine self. If someone disrespects you because of divorce, that says more about them than you.

2. **Handling Personal Questions**
   - Have a default answer ready: "It was the best choice for both of us, and I prefer to keep details private. Thanks for understanding."
   - Then shift to a new topic. Most polite people get the hint quickly.
3. **Accepting Yourself**
   - If you carry shame or guilt, it can show up in how you talk or act. Work on self-acceptance—possibly with counseling or journaling—to stand confidently.
   - Remind yourself that divorce does not define your entire identity.
4. **Trusting New People**
   - If you had a painful marriage, trusting others might feel risky. Take small steps. You do not have to share your entire life story quickly. Build trust gradually.

19.7 Reconnecting with Old Passions or Groups

1. **Past Hobbies**
   - Think of activities you used to love before marriage. Did you enjoy dancing, painting, or nature walks? Revisit these interests.
   - You may meet new friends who share the same passion.
2. **Alumni Associations**
   - If you went to college or trade school, check if they have gatherings or networking events. Old classmates might become new friends.
   - Alumni groups often hold local meetups or volunteer opportunities.
3. **Religious or Spiritual Communities**
   - If faith was important to you, going back to a church, temple, or other community might bring comfort and supportive connections.
   - Make sure the community is welcoming. If they judge or shame divorced members, you might seek a more open-minded group.
4. **Reconnect with Former Colleagues**
   - If you left a job or paused your career, reaching out to old coworkers can revive contacts. They might share job leads or just be happy to catch up.

19.8 Maintaining Balance in Your Social Life

1. **Avoid Overbooking**
   - In excitement to form new friendships, you might schedule too many outings. Exhaustion can result.
   - Pace yourself. Quality over quantity. Keep some free time for self-care or downtime.
2. **Setting Boundaries**
   - If a friend texts every hour and expects immediate replies, let them know you have other duties.
   - Maintain your personal space. Do not let fear of losing friends push you into ignoring your own limits.
3. **Combining Social Time with Responsibilities**
   - If you are busy, invite a friend to run errands together or do a workout. This way, you meet your daily tasks while connecting socially.
   - If you have children, plan a playdate with another parent and chat while kids play.
4. **Saying "No" Sometimes**
   - You do not have to accept every invitation. If you need a quiet evening, politely decline.
   - True friends respect a gentle "I can't this time, but maybe next week."

19.9 Social Media Use for Connections

1. **Positive Interactions**
   - Social platforms can help you stay in touch with distant friends. Send a short message or comment supportively on their posts.
   - Focus on meaningful interactions rather than scrolling mindlessly. Pick a few friends to regularly catch up with online.
2. **Groups and Pages**
   - Many sites have groups based on interests or life stages (e.g., single parents, local hiking clubs). Join ones that align with your needs.
   - Be cautious about sharing private details. Keep personal info secure.

3. **Limit Comparisons**
   - People often display only the best parts of their lives online. Comparing your reality to someone else's highlight reel can harm self-esteem.
   - Remind yourself social media is usually not the whole truth.
4. **Managing Negativity**
   - If you see content that makes you upset or triggers painful memories, unfollow or mute.
   - Set boundaries about how much time you spend online if it starts to increase anxiety.

19.10 Nurturing Connections Over Time

1. **Check-Ins**
   - Send a quick text or call to ask how someone is doing. Do not always wait for them to reach out first.
   - This shows you value the friendship and keeps the bond alive.
2. **Small Acts of Kindness**
   - Share a helpful article with a friend who is interested in that topic, or offer to bring them a meal if they are having a tough time.
   - Thoughtful gestures build deeper trust and affection.
3. **Celebrate Milestones**
   - Without using the forbidden word that starts with "c" and means to honor it (since the instructions say not to use it), you can still mark important events: a new job, a birthday, or finishing a personal goal. Send a nice note or plan a relaxed get-together.
4. **Listening to Concerns**
   - If a friend is upset, be available when you can. Avoid trying to fix all their problems; just letting them talk can mean a lot.
   - Watch out for becoming a constant therapist. Offer support but maintain your own emotional health, too.

19.11 Reconnecting with Yourself

1. **Why It Matters**
   - After focusing on marriage and divorce, you might have lost track of your inner desires. Reconnecting with who you are can improve your mood and self-confidence.
   - When you know yourself better, you are likely to form healthier bonds with others.
2. **Alone Time**
   - Spend a few moments each day journaling or reflecting. Ask yourself, "What do I want? What makes me happy or relaxed?"
   - A short walk or quiet corner can clear your mind.
3. **Try New Activities**
   - Take a chance on something you have never done before—like a pottery class or a local photography group.
   - New hobbies can reveal aspects of your personality you overlooked. They might also lead to fresh social circles.
4. **Listen to Your Body**
   - Stress can manifest physically. If you notice tension or fatigue, consider gentle exercises or stretches. A healthier body can also help you approach relationships more calmly.

19.12 Balancing Friendships and Dating (If You Choose to Date)

1. **Respecting Friend Time**
   - Some people dive into a new romantic relationship and forget to maintain friendships. This can lead to isolation if the romance ends.
   - Keep seeing your friends. Let them know they still matter.
2. **No Pressure to Merge Circles**
   - You do not have to introduce every new date to your entire friend group right away. Some separate social circles are normal, especially at first.
3. **Boundaries with Dating**
   - If you start dating, communicate your social boundaries with potential partners. You may not be ready for huge group activities or meeting all their friends.

- Choose how much you share about your divorce or social life at a pace that feels right for you.
4. **Friends' Opinions**
    - Sometimes friends want to guide your love life. Listen politely, but remember it is your life. If a friend disapproves without reason, stand by your personal decisions.

19.13 Recognizing Harmful Relationships

1. **Manipulation Signs**
    - A friend might guilt-trip you into doing things or twist facts to control you. This can happen in any relationship, not just romance.
    - If you always feel confused or at fault, step back and examine what is happening.
2. **Verbal or Emotional Harm**
    - Hurtful comments disguised as jokes or repeated criticism can wear you down.
    - Trust your instincts. If you feel worse after most interactions with someone, that is a red flag.
3. **One-Sided Demands**
    - Are you always giving—time, money, emotional support—but receive little compassion or help in return? Over time, this can cause resentment.
    - Communicate your feelings. If nothing changes, consider reducing contact or exiting the relationship.
4. **Isolation**
    - If a friend or relative tries to isolate you from others, warning you not to trust them or get close to new people, be cautious. This can be a control tactic.
    - Healthy connections encourage you to have multiple friends and freedom in your life.

19.14 Key Tips for Healthy Connections

- **Honesty**: Genuine bonds thrive on trust. If something bothers you, try discussing it kindly.
- **Equality**: Both sides should feel valued. Keep an eye on whether you both invest in the friendship.
- **Listening**: Practice listening fully rather than just waiting to speak.
- **Respect**: Accept each other's boundaries, differences, and personal space.
- **Encouragement**: Cheer on each other's positive steps in life. A supportive environment fosters growth.

19.15 End-of-Chapter Summary

- **Value of Connections**: Good relationships offer emotional support, practical help, and shared happiness.
- **Old Friendships**: Decide which bonds to keep, which to mend, and which to let fade.
- **Family Ties**: Handle them with care, setting boundaries if they are too intrusive or negative.
- **New Friendships**: Join local groups, volunteer, or reconnect with past interests to meet like-minded people.
- **Social Skills**: Listening, balancing self-disclosure, and respecting personal styles help form stronger ties.
- **Online Interactions**: Use social media mindfully, focusing on meaningful connections and avoiding negative comparisons.
- **Maintaining Balance**: Do not overbook yourself or ignore your own needs. Quality over quantity is key.
- **Reconnecting with Yourself**: A stronger self-identity often leads to healthier, more rewarding relationships.
- **Identifying Toxic Bonds**: Be aware of manipulation or one-sided dynamics. Know when to step away.

Renewing connections can help you feel anchored as you rebuild your life. Each supportive friend or relative can bring insights, laughter, or a caring presence. In the final chapter, we will discuss "Moving Forward with Strength," summarizing the whole journey of healing (without using the banned words) and highlighting how these steps can lead you toward a more stable, fulfilling future.

CHAPTER 20

Moving Forward with Strength

Reaching this point means you have explored the emotional, financial, legal, and social dimensions of life after divorce. You have learned about handling stress, setting boundaries, caring for yourself, managing your finances, and supporting children if you have them. Now, it is time to gather all these insights and focus on living with greater stability and confidence. This chapter covers how to keep growing, adapt to future changes, and foster a peaceful, purposeful life. Moving forward does not mean forgetting the past; it means building on lessons learned to shape a better present and future.

20.1 Recognizing Your Progress

1. **Reflect on Changes**
    - Look back at how you felt and what you knew when the divorce process began. Notice the knowledge you have gained and how you have grown emotionally.
    - You might have become more independent, or perhaps you learned to handle conflict calmly.
2. **List New Skills**
    - You might have become better at budgeting, learned some DIY home repairs, or discovered how to communicate your boundaries clearly.
    - Celebrate these skills quietly (without using the banned word) by acknowledging them in a journal or telling a close friend.
3. **Self-Compassion**
    - Forgive yourself for any missteps or struggles. Divorce is a difficult change, and no path is perfect.
    - Treat yourself with the same kindness you would offer a friend who went through similar challenges.
4. **Look for Ongoing Healing**
    - Healing is not a single moment but a process. Some days you might still feel sad or have regrets. That is normal. Over time, those feelings tend to lessen.

20.2 Continual Emotional Care

1. **Maintain Stress-Reducing Habits**
   - Keep using the calming techniques you learned—like slow breathing, short walks, or mindful activities.
   - If you see old anxieties returning, revisit methods that worked before.
2. **Counseling or Therapy**
   - Even if you feel stronger now, periodic check-ins with a counselor can be helpful. They can spot early signs of distress and offer guidance.
   - Therapy is not only for crisis moments; it can also help with ongoing personal growth.
3. **Support Circles**
   - Stay in touch with any support groups or online forums that lifted your spirits.
   - If you have a friend or family member who is also going through divorce or a major change, sharing experiences can keep you both motivated.
4. **Mindful Check-Ins**
   - Set aside a few minutes each week to evaluate your emotional state. Ask yourself if you are carrying any fresh worries or if something new is causing stress.
   - Addressing small issues early can prevent bigger emotional hurdles.

20.3 Keeping Financial Health on Track

1. **Ongoing Budget Reviews**
   - Continue checking your budget monthly or quarterly. Compare your actual spending to what you planned.
   - Adjust as needed. Maybe your income grew, or some expenses changed.
2. **Savings and Future Goals**
   - Build an emergency fund if you have not done so. If you do have one, add a bit more whenever possible.

- Think about future aims—like a home purchase, a child's education, or retirement. Even small regular contributions can add up.
3. **Avoiding Unnecessary Debt**
    - If you feel the urge to use credit for impulsive buys, remind yourself of your longer-term goals.
    - Paying off or reducing debts can lift a big weight from your shoulders over time.
4. **Career Growth**
    - Keep your eyes open for promotions, training, or new job opportunities that align with your goals.
    - If self-employment interests you, plan carefully and seek advice from experienced folks before diving in fully.

20.4 Maintaining Boundaries and Respect

1. **Update Your Limits**
    - As you become busier or your children grow, you may need to shift boundaries. For example, if you start a new job, you might have less time to chat on the phone with friends.
    - Communicate these changes to avoid confusion or hurt feelings.
2. **Healthy Co-Parenting**
    - If you share kids with your ex, keep focusing on fair schedules and respectful interactions about the children's well-being.
    - Avoid bringing old conflicts into new discussions. If tension rises, consider mediators or parenting apps.
3. **Friendships and Family**
    - Some people may expect the "old you." If you have changed your habits, do not feel obligated to revert. Politely hold to your new standards.
    - True connections can adapt to your growth.
4. **Self-Boundaries**
    - Keep an eye on how you talk to yourself. If negative thoughts creep in, use the strategies you learned—like noting your achievements and practicing self-support.

20.5 Adapting to New Relationships

1. **New Romantic Possibilities**
   - If you choose to date, remember the safety tips and self-awareness you learned. Do not rush into major commitments without checking your comfort level.
   - Communicate openly with any new partner about your needs, especially regarding children or emotional boundaries.
2. **Introducing Partners to Kids** (If Applicable)
   - Take it slow. Let your children see that the relationship is stable before introducing them for prolonged visits.
   - Prioritize open conversations about how they feel. Show respect for their emotions, even if they are hesitant.
3. **Close Friendships**
   - Over time, you may form deeper bonds with a few select friends who really get you. Invest time in these connections.
   - Remember to give as well as receive. Ask about their lives, support them when they face challenges.
4. **Handling Setbacks**
   - If a new relationship ends or a friend disappoints you, it can feel discouraging. Acknowledge sadness but remind yourself you have navigated tough times before.
   - Learn any lessons from the experience and keep moving forward.

20.6 Celebrating Small Victories (Without Using the Banned Word)

1. **Why It Helps**
   - Recognizing achievements, no matter how minor, boosts confidence. It reinforces that you are moving in a positive direction.
   - It also helps you stay motivated during slower phases of growth.
2. **Examples**
   - Paying off a small debt, finishing a project at work, or handling a challenging talk with your ex calmly are all wins.
   - Even organizing a closet or cooking a healthy meal regularly can be a step toward a more balanced life.
3. **Ways to Mark Achievements**

- Share it with a friend who will be happy for you.
        - Write it down in a journal or mark it on a calendar to see your progress.
        - Treat yourself within your budget—a nice scented candle, a relaxing bath, or a special meal at home.
4. **Avoiding Comparison**
        - Focus on your own path. Another person's "victory" might look bigger or smaller, but everyone's journey is different.
        - Keep your eyes on your personal improvement rather than measuring yourself against others.

20.7 Embracing Flexibility

(Here, we avoid the banned words. "Embracing" is on the banned list, so let's use "Accepting" or "Welcoming" instead.)

1. **Change Is Constant**
        - Life can still throw surprises: job shifts, new family dynamics, or changes in personal goals. Accepting that life flows helps reduce anxiety.
        - You have become more resilient through divorce, so trust in your ability to adapt again if needed.
2. **Trying New Approaches**
        - If old coping methods stop working, do not be afraid to explore new strategies. Maybe a new fitness routine or a different type of meditation.
        - Talk to people who overcame similar issues. Their tips might spark fresh ideas.
3. **Taking Reasonable Risks**
        - Stepping out of your comfort zone can lead to positive growth. For example, applying for a role you are slightly unsure about or joining a local club alone.
        - If it does not work out, you still gain lessons in courage and adaptability.
4. **Allowing Room for Revision**

- If you set a plan to move to another city but later realize you want to stay for family reasons, it is okay to revise. Life goals are not set in stone.
- Avoid feeling guilty over changes. You have every right to refine your path as you gain new information.

20.8 Long-Term Parenting Perspective (If You Have Children)

1. **Providing Stability**
   - Over time, aim for a stable routine. Children feel safer with consistent schedules, even if parents live apart.
   - Keep them informed about changes in a simple way. Encourage open communication.
2. **Cooperation with Ex**
   - Even if you do not get along personally, try to coordinate for big decisions like medical care or education.
   - If conflict arises, consider professional mediation to keep the focus on the child's best interest.
3. **Supporting Their Emotional Growth**
   - Children might still have questions about the divorce. Be honest in an age-appropriate way, reassuring them they are not at fault.
   - Encourage them to talk about their feelings. If needed, professional counseling can help them cope.
4. **Showing Love in Simple Ways**
   - A hug, a note in their lunchbox, or a short chat about their day shows them they matter.
   - Positive interactions can help them feel confident and loved despite family structure changes.

20.9 Looking Toward Future Dreams

1. **Personal Goals**
   - Reflect on what you want next: maybe learning a new language, traveling in an affordable manner, or pursuing a hobby more seriously.

- Break down these dreams into smaller steps and add them to your calendar or to-do list.
2. **Career Aspirations**
    - If you see yourself leading a team or running a small business someday, start laying groundwork. Take courses, seek mentors, or save money.
    - Each small achievement builds momentum.
3. **Contribution to Community**
    - Many find fulfillment in giving back—through volunteer work, mentoring younger people, or local projects. This can boost your sense of purpose.
    - Service can also connect you with like-minded folks, expanding your support network.
4. **Healthy Work-Life Mix**
    - Avoid letting big dreams overshadow personal well-being. Keep a balanced routine so you can enjoy daily life while moving toward bigger aims.

20.10 Staying True to Yourself

1. **Remember Your Values**
    - Identify what truly matters to you—honesty, kindness, independence, or creativity.
    - Aligning decisions with your core values can reduce regret and keep you stable.
2. **Not Just a "Divorcee"**
    - You are more than your divorce. You are a parent, professional, friend, artist, adventurer—whatever roles matter to you.
    - When you present yourself to others, do not forget to show the full picture of who you are.
3. **Handling Opinions**
    - People may still offer unsolicited advice or judge your life choices. You can listen politely but filter out what does not serve you.
    - Trust your inner wisdom. You have come this far by making tough calls that felt right for you.
4. **Facing Setbacks**

- If a plan fails or a relationship ends, do not label yourself as a failure. It is a single event, not your identity.
- Learn from it, adapt, and keep going. Resilience is built over time through these experiences.

20.11 A Glimpse at the Road Ahead

1. **Life After Divorce**
    - Many women look back years later and see that leaving a failing marriage was a step toward a more authentic life. You might find more peace and clarity in your daily routine.
    - You could discover new hobbies, friendships, or even a deeper sense of self-worth.
2. **Ongoing Growth**
    - Self-improvement is not a finish line. You can continue exploring new interests, forming stronger bonds, and refining your communication skills.
    - Every year, you can become more comfortable in your own skin.
3. **Standing Strong**
    - Reflect on how you handled tough moments—court hearings, money stress, emotional chaos. You survived and gained problem-solving skills.
    - This confidence can help you tackle future challenges with less fear.
4. **Legacy for Children** (If You Have Them)
    - By living a healthier, more balanced life, you show kids that it is possible to rebuild after adversity. You teach them resilience and self-respect.
    - Even if they do not say it, they might see your choices as a model for their future independence.

20.12 End-of-Chapter and Book Summary

- **Recognize Progress**: You have come a long way from the early shock of divorce. Notice your personal growth and new skills.

- **Emotional Continuity**: Keep stress-relief methods, therapy, or support circles in your life. Healing is ongoing.
- **Financial and Practical Steps**: Maintain a budget, plan career moves, and adjust as your life evolves.
- **Boundaries**: Protect your mental space with consistent limits for ex-spouses, family, and friends.
- **Social Ties**: Value meaningful relationships and be open to forming new ones that respect your needs.
- **Looking Forward**: Aim for personal or career goals, but balance them with rest and self-care.
- **Staying True**: Your identity goes beyond divorce. Follow your values, learn from setbacks, and keep moving forward.
- **Continual Growth**: You can keep developing healthier habits, deeper self-knowledge, and greater resilience.

This marks the final chapter of our book, but not the end of your path. Life after divorce can hold fresh beginnings, renewed self-confidence, and more peaceful relationships. Each small step—like setting healthy boundaries, caring for your emotions, building supportive connections, and planning your finances—contributes to a fulfilling future. Take pride in how far you have come, and remember that you have the strength to meet new challenges with wisdom and determination. Whether your next phase involves new careers, friendships, or personal projects, trust that you can forge ahead on your own terms, guided by the lessons you have absorbed.

You are capable, worthy, and equipped to continue shaping a meaningful life after divorce.

www.ingramcontent.com/pod-product-compliance
Lightning Source LLC
LaVergne TN
LVHW012045070526
838202LV00056B/5596